Men'sHealth. **MAGAZINE** *Prese*

Uncommon Knowledge

Hundreds of How-To Tips from *Your Favorite Celebs!*

Edited by David Zinczenko
Illustrations by Dan Krovatin
Introduction by Greg Gutfeld

RODALE

To my mother, Jan.
You've always been so supportive.
Now please buy 20,000 copies of this book.
—Dave

Illustrations by Dan Krovatin (except glue and clamp illustrations, p. 53, by Steven Noble)

Cover and interior design by Shelia Monaghan

Cover photographs by Darryl Estrine/Outline (Hugh M. Hefner), Everett Collection (Alex Trebek, Dick Clark), and John McDonough/Icon SMI (Dennis Rodman)

Library of Congress Cataloging-in-Publication Data

Uncommon knowledge : hundreds of how-to tips from your favorite celebs! / edited by
    David Zinczenko ; introduction by Greg Gutfeld ; illustrations by Dan Krovatin
        p.   cm.
    ISBN 1–57954–291–3 paperback
    1. Life skills—Humor.   2. Celebrities—Humor.   I. Zinczenko, David.
PN6231.L49 U63   2000
818'.540208—dc21   00–023905

Distributed to the book trade by St. Martin's Press

2 4 6 8 10 9 7 5 3 1   paperback

Visit us on the Web at www.menshealth.com, or call us toll-free at (800) 848-4735.

WE **INSPIRE** AND **ENABLE** PEOPLE TO IMPROVE
THEIR LIVES AND THE WORLD AROUND THEM

Contents

Introduction

It used to be that if you wanted to learn how to do something well, the last person you'd think of asking was a celebrity. If anything, when you ask the rich and famous, you learn how *not* to do stuff well. Think about it: Stars are great at screwing things up. In the last few years, for example, celebs have taught us how not to drive a sports car (Kelsey Grammer), how not to mentor young talent (Bill Clinton), how not to handle yourself in public (Pee Wee Herman, George Michael, the entire Sheen family), and how not to settle disputes without killing dozens of innocent people (Janet Reno).

But *Men's Health* changed that. *Men's Health* is a magazine built on practical, solid advice that actually works. While we don't give a damn about Jim Carrey's angst or George Clooney's pants (we'll leave that to those fine lads at *Esquire*), we wondered if it might be possible to cull some useful info from famous guys we liked.

And so we did, in our back-page column called "Uncommon Knowledge." For each issue, we asked a celebrity to teach us something only he could teach us. Don King showed us how to train a boxer, Pete Sampras told us how to swat flies, Jerry Springer said all that could be said on how to clean out gutters, and Ray Charles pointed out the nuances of selecting sunglasses.

After 5 years of doing this—gaining wisdom from guys who aren't used to dispensing it—we realized that we had enough stuff for a really cool book. Each one of these articles originally appeared on the back page of *Men's Health* magazine, skillfully edited by David Zinczenko.

It turns out that every guy's got something to teach you. Even if the guy is, well, a celebrity. True, some would rather give their opinions on global warming and the spotted owl—but you won't find those here.

What's surprising is that even Dweezil Zappa can teach you something.

What's not surprising is that neither Alec Baldwin nor Ed Begley Jr. knew anything worth knowing.

But you knew that.

Greg Gutfeld
Editor-in-Chief, *Men's Health* magazine

DR. HENRY HEIMLICH

How to Stop Yourself from Choking

Life is a lot like golf. It's usually long, it's often boring, and there's a lot of waiting around. But then there comes a moment when everything's on the line—you're staring down that fairway, facing Sudden Death. In times like this, defeat is just too hard to swallow.

Here's a story that'll bring a lump to your throat. About 25 years ago, I invented a certain technique. A maneuver, so to speak. Now my name hangs next to the kitchen door of every all-you-can-eat restaurant in America. But get this: I've never had a chance to save even one choker using the Heimlich maneuver—and I don't get royalties when anyone else does. Sometimes my friends suspect that I lurk in restaurants, hoping to free a stuck sirloin from a clogged glottis. But even though I haven't used the Heimlich maneuver on anyone, that doesn't mean I can't save you from choking, in certain circumstances.

1 VISUALIZE THE MANEUVER

You have to visualize your success to make it happen, whether it's extracting a chunk of chuck steak from a friend's throat or executing a 50-foot putt.

But don't take all day for your fantasy. A choking victim can succumb in just 4 minutes, and most golf courses have penalties for slow play. If you live your winning moment in advance, you'll be able to recall that feeling of confidence and inevitable success when the chips are down.

2 WORK THE DIAPHRAGM

When the whole kit and caboodle is on the line, you can always count on an annoying bystander to disrupt your concentration.

Great athletes avoid choking under pressure by blocking distractions—hecklers, fans, in-laws. One way to do this is to concentrate on your breathing. Oxygenate yourself by taking a few deep belly breaths—stomach out, chest in—to relieve stress. Counting backward is another tactic that might help you relax.

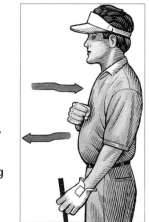

3 KNOW WHEN TO SEEK HELP

In a tough spot, you need every advantage.

Even imaginary ones will do. Some runners envision a rope tied around their waist, pulling them forward. Weight lifters might pretend that their barbell is on a track, locking them into perfect form. For me, sinking a high-pressure putt is a mind game as well. I like to think of the putter as a pendulum that swings back and forth smoothly (inset). An image like this can give you the confidence to maneuver your little sphere right down a clown's throat. Or, if need be, right back out of it.

HUGH M. HEFNER

How to Pick a Melon

What is it about a beautiful, round, ripe melon that spikes a guy's appetite, makes him want more? Truth is, if the day's warm and sunny and full of promise, one melon won't do. Because getting your hands on one just makes you want two.

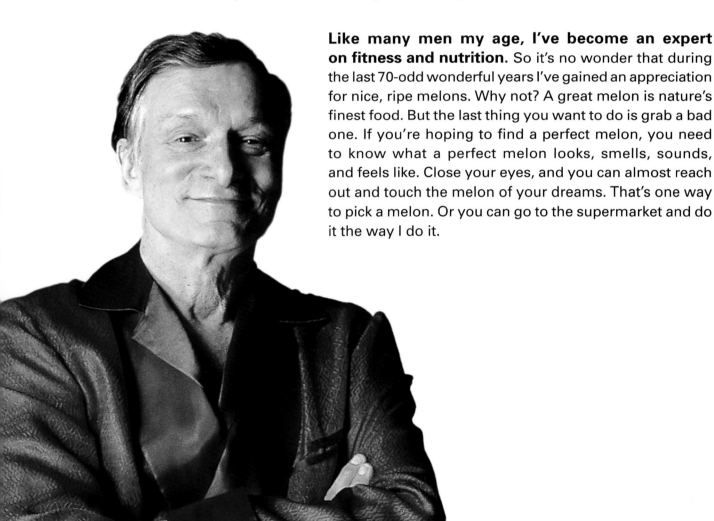

Like many men my age, I've become an expert on fitness and nutrition. So it's no wonder that during the last 70-odd wonderful years I've gained an appreciation for nice, ripe melons. Why not? A great melon is nature's finest food. But the last thing you want to do is grab a bad one. If you're hoping to find a perfect melon, you need to know what a perfect melon looks, smells, sounds, and feels like. Close your eyes, and you can almost reach out and touch the melon of your dreams. That's one way to pick a melon. Or you can go to the supermarket and do it the way I do it.

1 KNOW YOUR MELONS

The first thing you need to know is what you're looking for.

The best way to judge a melon is by its shape, size, and color. A good, ripe cantaloupe, for example, should have a cream-colored netting on the skin, and the background should be a golden yellow shade. A honeydew should be smooth and satiny, with a cream-colored skin. And a watermelon is perfect if it's a nice deep green with lighter stripes.

2 GET YOUR HANDS ON 'EM

Don't be afraid to put your hands on a melon and give it a good squeeze.

I've always preferred to use a palms-out touch, although plenty of other guys like to feel the heft of the melon in their hands. Either way, don't squeeze too hard! It just makes the produce manager mad. Instead, gently press the melon at the blossom end, where it was attached to the plant. It should give without losing its firmness. If it's too soft to the touch, it's past its peak. Ripe melons have a shelf life of no more than 2 weeks. After that, they get mushy and lose their pert, rounded shape. Artificial melons—the kind made of plastic and used for display—always look perfect. But they aren't real, so who needs them?

3 SNIFF AND SHAKE

Another great way to determine if the melon's any good is to give it a sniff.

It should smell sweet, not moldy or dusty. And while you want to shake a good martini to a rumba rhythm, a melon should be done to a waltz. 1-2-3, 1-2-3. And, while you're waltzing with the melon, hold it to your ear and listen for seeds shaking inside. If you hear any rattling, you're dancing with the wrong melon. During the spring and summer especially, a good grocery has many, many melons to offer. Be patient and you'll find the perfect melon for you.

DENNIS RODMAN

How to Talk to a Barber

Nothing lends a man more respect and credibility than a subtle and stylish haircut.

My hair is a precious commodity. Unlike a lot of NBA stars, who prefer to go without hair, I've made an indulgence of the elegant turf that rides my dome. It's my calling card, my trademark. So that's why I take extra care in choosing the guy who's going to cut it, shape it, fade it, and paint it. One slip of the scissors, and I gotta wear it for everyone to see, night after night. But you don't need a ritzy joint with ferns in the windows. Just go to a barber. A place where there's always hair on the floor and the sports page within reach.

1 LOOK FOR THE BIG POLE

That red-, white-, and blue-striped pole out front means you're dealing with a real barber—not a "stylist."

Barbers understand men, and they speak our language. No unsettling talk about mousse or highlights. Plus, you can have a conversation in a barbershop. If a guy two chairs down says something like "Why can't Rodman shoot?" you can engage him in constructive conversation without worrying about bothering anyone. Also, with a barber, you don't need to make an appointment weeks in advance, and you don't have to squeeze past the manicure table to get to a chair. As a rule, avoid any place where the guy cutting your hair has only one name. In fact, avoid anybody who has only one name.

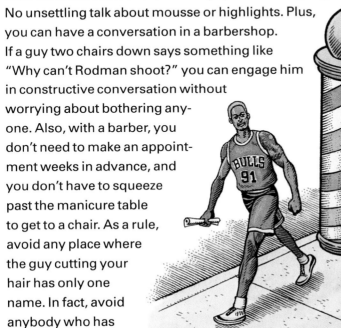

2 SHOW, DON'T TELL

Barbers have their own way of talking about hair.

Unless you really know the difference between "tapered" (short in the back, longer on the top) and "layered" (each strand of hair is the same length), don't try to talk in fancy barber-speak. Instead, take along a photograph that shows the look you want.

And don't be afraid to ask questions. Is there any scalp showing in the back? Is the hairline receding? Do you think purple is really my best color? Be up front with your barber, and chances are he'll have a solution to whatever's been nagging you.

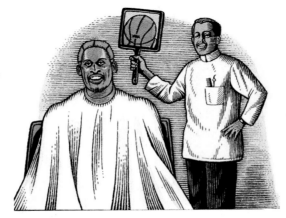

3 ALWAYS LOOK BACK

After your barber is finished cutting, make sure he shows you the back of your head.

A lot of barbers will try to spare you the embarrassment of seeing some skin. But let's face it, while *you* may not see it, everyone else will. Even when you're 6-foot-8.

OLIVER NORTH

How to Survive a Grilling

Nothing defines a man more than his ability to handle life's meaty questions. So when things start heating up in your backyard, grab a spatula. It pays to know how to keep your cool when you're being raked over the coals.

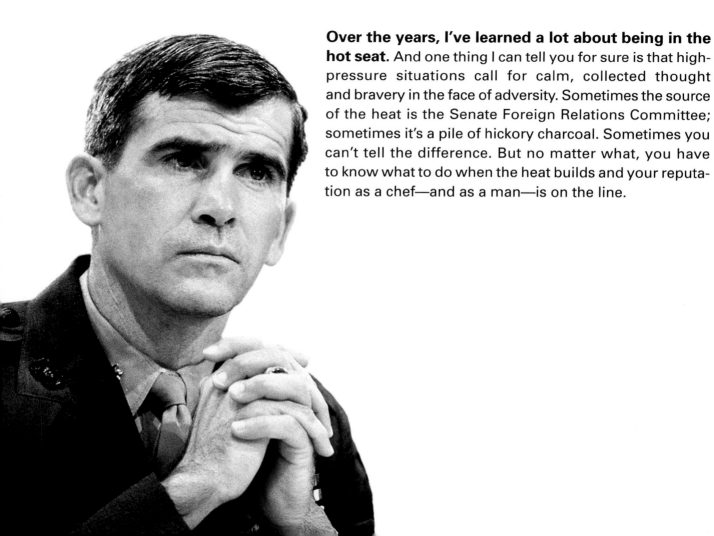

Over the years, I've learned a lot about being in the hot seat. And one thing I can tell you for sure is that high-pressure situations call for calm, collected thought and bravery in the face of adversity. Sometimes the source of the heat is the Senate Foreign Relations Committee; sometimes it's a pile of hickory charcoal. Sometimes you can't tell the difference. But no matter what, you have to know what to do when the heat builds and your reputation as a chef—and as a man—is on the line.

1 STACK THE EVIDENCE

Barbecues don't just happen. You can see them coming— sometimes days in advance.

So be ready: Most pregrill activity involves tedious chopping, skinning, mixing—maybe even shredding. Arrange everything in the sequence in which it will be grilled. The actual cooking is a brief, dramatic burst of fiery activity in a smoky hellhole fit only for the brave of heart—and those who have prepared properly. Keep the prep work undercover, out of the public eye. Remember: What they don't know won't hurt them.

2 CONTROL THE HEAT

A friendly fire has two parts:

One hot, heaping pile of coals for searing the meat, and another not-so-heaping pile for cooking it. Light the small one, wait 10 minutes, then light the large one. When the big pile is red hot, it's time for meat to meet metal. Sear burgers for 5 minutes per side. With chicken, sear the skin, then cook the flesh thoroughly. For steak, massage in a little olive oil mixed with soy sauce and grated garlic, then sear the meat hot and fast. A rare 2-inch steak should be grilled about 8 minutes per side. Vegetables? Who cares? Cook 'em till they wilt like a liberal on *Crossfire*.

3 DOUSE THE FLAMES

If your steaks are ablaze, calmly cover the grill to smother the flames.

Then carefully raise the rack and spread the coals. If you've got a towering inferno, pluck your food off the grill and mist the fire with a spray bottle filled with beer. If it's too late, scrape off the offending matter and just pass out the beer. Remember, when it comes to handling the heat, never guess, never explain, never apologize.

CHEECH MARIN

How to Roll a Joint

When your knees, shoulders, or elbows are rattling like a loose bag, take a second to roll your own. Sometimes it's the only way to keep from getting busted.

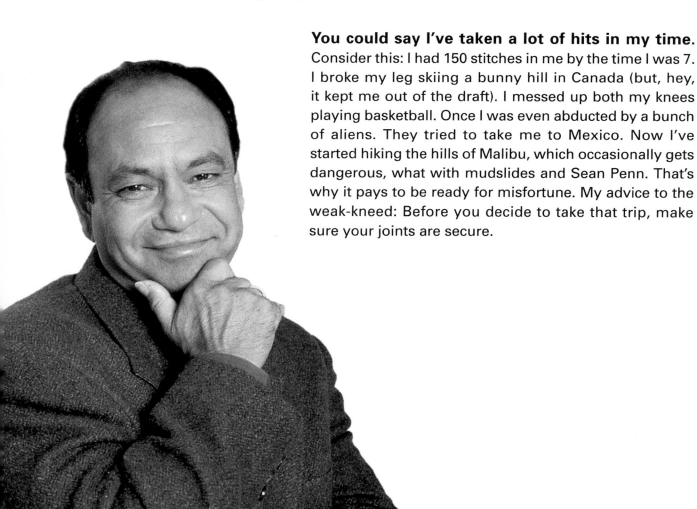

You could say I've taken a lot of hits in my time. Consider this: I had 150 stitches in me by the time I was 7. I broke my leg skiing a bunny hill in Canada (but, hey, it kept me out of the draft). I messed up both my knees playing basketball. Once I was even abducted by a bunch of aliens. They tried to take me to Mexico. Now I've started hiking the hills of Malibu, which occasionally gets dangerous, what with mudslides and Sean Penn. That's why it pays to be ready for misfortune. My advice to the weak-kneed: Before you decide to take that trip, make sure your joints are secure.

1 ROLL A BIG ONE

When you're talking about a big joint, like the knee, you need to use a lot of wrap to protect it properly.

Most elastic bandages come in 2-, 3-, and 6-inch widths. Pick the big one. Otherwise you won't cover enough of your leg to do any good.

Start by laying one end of the bandage against the front of your shin, about 6 inches below the knee; then begin unrolling it, round and round, up your leg. Wrap right over the kneecap and keep going. When you reach a point about 6 inches above the knee, wrap your way down again. That way your joint gets the benefit of two snug layers of support.

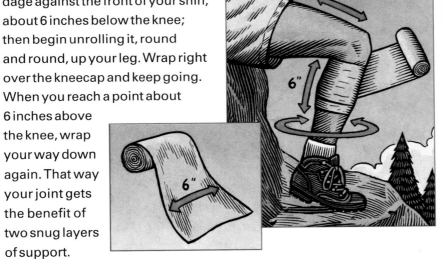

2 DON'T WRAP TOO TIGHTLY

After you're finished wrapping, slide a finger under the bandage to check the fit.

If you can't do this, your joint is wrapped too tightly. This cuts down on circulation, and that can be a drag. Circulation's important when you're talking joints. Circulation's good. Unwrap the joint and start again.

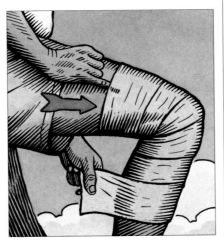

3 EMPLOY A CLIP

The final joint point: When you're at the very end, use a clip.

The best kind is a butterfly clip— though a roach clip will work in a pinch, too. To keep the bandage snug for a couple of hours, apply some athletic tape over the clip to prevent it from popping off. If your bones start getting creaky, as mine have, these wrapping techniques can help keep you healthy and active. After all, you don't want your body to go to pot.

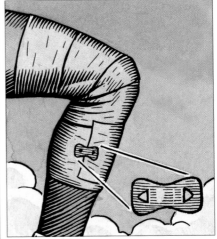

MIKE WALLACE

How to Carve Up a Turkey

The lights are on, the family video camera is rolling, and all eyes are on you. Are you going to come through in the clutch, or is that bird in the hot seat going to get the better of you?

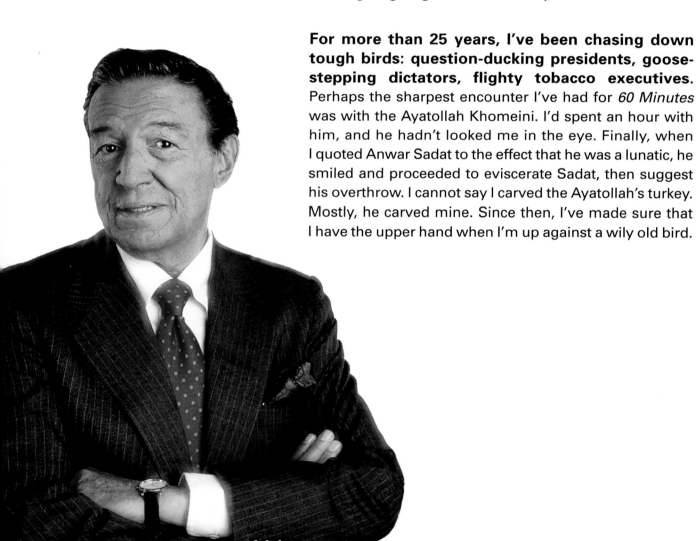

For more than 25 years, I've been chasing down tough birds: question-ducking presidents, goose-stepping dictators, flighty tobacco executives. Perhaps the sharpest encounter I've had for *60 Minutes* was with the Ayatollah Khomeini. I'd spent an hour with him, and he hadn't looked me in the eye. Finally, when I quoted Anwar Sadat to the effect that he was a lunatic, he smiled and proceeded to eviscerate Sadat, then suggest his overthrow. I cannot say I carved the Ayatollah's turkey. Mostly, he carved mine. Since then, I've made sure that I have the upper hand when I'm up against a wily old bird.

1 INTRODUCE YOURSELF

To make sure your quarry is ready for carving, throw open the oven door, shine some bright lights inside, and introduce yourself by reaching in and shaking the drumstick.

If it jiggles and moves away from the body easily, you're ready for prime time. You can also go the more reliable route by plunging an Insta Read thermometer into the bird's heart. If the temperature is 180°F in the thickest part of the breast, your turkey's ready to be served. But don't carve your bird right away—let him sweat it out in the next room for 20 to 30 minutes. If you go for the kill too quickly, the meat will be too hot and turn to mush.

2 PIN HIM DOWN

Once your turkey's goose is cooked, so to speak, place him in his most vulnerable position by facing his neck to your left if you're right-handed [A].

To make sure the bird won't go anywhere, cut off a leg first. Grasp the drumstick and press the leg away from the body, then use the point of your knife to sever the thigh joint, taking off the entire leg [B]. Don't make the amateur mistake of trying to break off the drumstick first. It's an ugly battle, and your quarry is likely to slip out of your grasp and wriggle right off the hot seat.

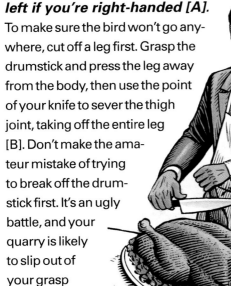

3 MAKE A MEAL OUT OF HIM

Now go for his heart.

Stick a fork into his wing to steady him and make a long horizontal cut—in a large, bold stroke—above the wing and through the breast to the ribs [C]. Now start cutting straight down, from halfway up the breast [D]. When the knife reaches the horizontal cut, the meat will fall free, and eventually you'll pull the whole story out of the pile of bones the turkey's left behind.

CHRISTOPHER DARDEN

How to Prepare a Case

When you have to travel far to seek redress, you need to make sure that your suits and your briefs—and the rest of your case—come through without a hitch. Here's how to call your whole wardrobe to order.

In the past few years, I've done an awful lot of traveling, what with publicity appearances, lectures, book signings, and the like. And the one thing I've learned is that the rules of dressing to impress remain the same whether you're arguing a case, pursuing a witness, or pitching an outstanding new piece of literature. You need to give the best accounting of yourself, and you can't do this if your clothes are wrinkled and look as if you slept in them the night before. A well-prepared case will keep your clothes from being jostled and crumpled—even when you're running through airports.

1 PUT YOUR BEST FOOT FORWARD

Because jury members often sit above the courtroom floor, in the jury box, they have a clear view of your ensemble, including your shoes.

As any woman will tell you, there's nothing worse than a man in run-down shoes. Worn shoes signify that you're not careful with minor details—a bad idea when you're trying to explain the intricacies of DNA testing. Shield the shoes from damage by stuffing your socks into them, then place them along the back edge of the bottom of the suitcase. This way, you won't leave incriminating footprints all over the place.

2 PROTECT YOUR MATERIAL WITNESSES

Pack a nice, conservative suit, nothing too showy.

You want to blend in with a jury, and a funny-looking lavender or mustard suit will make you stand out like Mark Fuhrman at an NAACP convention. Lay your trousers in the suitcase with the legs extending outside the case [A]. Pack your shirts facing each other, preferably in dry-cleaner bags. (If there's no fabric-to-fabric contact, there won't be wrinkles.) Next, pack your T-shirts, vests, and sweaters [B]. Once you have a full caseload—as you should to keep garments from shifting—fold the trouser legs over everything [C]. Roll your ties and slip them, and your belts, wherever you can fit them in. Throw your gloves into the case at this point, too. Trust me, they'll fit.

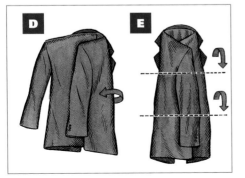

3 PRESENT A WINNING SUIT

The suit jacket is the most difficult piece to pack.

Wrinkle it and you'll have a sartorial case of "prior restraint" on your hands. Bad stuff. To prevent creases, use the old tuck-and-roll: Put the coat facedown on the bed. Fold one front side of the coat back to the rear center seam [D]. Then fold back the other half and tuck it under the opposite shoulder [E]. Fold down the top third of the coat, then fold it once more. Then, slip the coat into a plastic bag and place it in the suitcase.

How to Build a Raft

Sometimes life can leave you stranded and thinking that all hope is lost. But the solution to your problem might be right there in front of you—if you can see the forest for the trees.

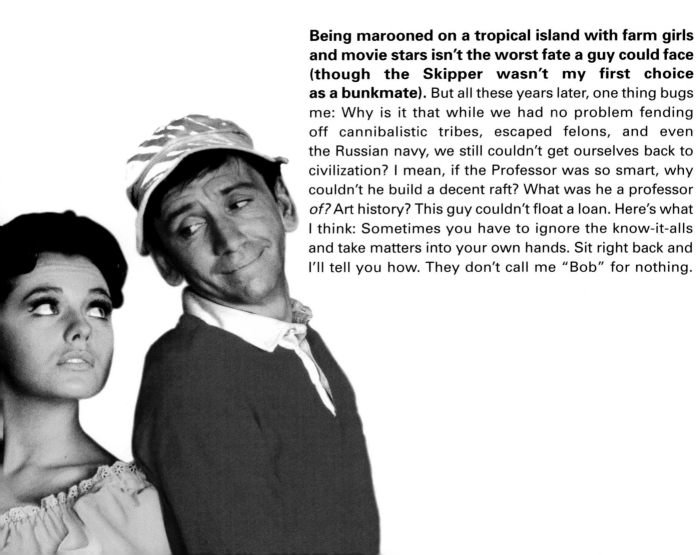

Being marooned on a tropical island with farm girls and movie stars isn't the worst fate a guy could face (though the Skipper wasn't my first choice as a bunkmate). But all these years later, one thing bugs me: Why is it that while we had no problem fending off cannibalistic tribes, escaped felons, and even the Russian navy, we still couldn't get ourselves back to civilization? I mean, if the Professor was so smart, why couldn't he build a decent raft? What was he a professor *of?* Art history? This guy couldn't float a loan. Here's what I think: Sometimes you have to ignore the know-it-alls and take matters into your own hands. Sit right back and I'll tell you how. They don't call me "Bob" for nothing.

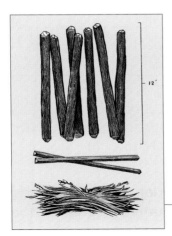

1 BE RESOURCEFUL
You don't need a Ph.D. to build a raft.
And you don't need to be a millionaire. All you need is a hand ax and a bunch of dead wood. Cut a half dozen or so 12-foot-long dry logs—thick ones, about 12 inches in diameter—and two smaller logs, say 7 or 8 feet long and 4 to 6 inches across. Look for something you can use as a kind of twine—such as willow withes, fibrous bark, or even coarse seaweed—to tie the logs together.

2 MAKE THE CUT
Take the big logs and place them side by side until you have a 12-by-7-foot platform.
This is big enough for a stable raft that can carry you and Mary Ann (sorry, Ginger). About a foot-and-a-half from the ends of each log, cut small "dovetail" notches 2 inches deep and wider at the bottom than at the top. I could explain this process, but never mind. Just look at the drawing.

3 GET HITCHED
Line up the logs so the notches are even with each other.
Cut the smaller logs into three-sided pieces of wood, then slide them through the inverted notches to connect the logs. Tie these crosspieces in place with the seaweed. Finally, cover the raft with brush to provide dry footing and a place for baggage (pack extra—you never know when a 3-hour tour will turn into 30 years in syndication). Put the stuff toward the forward end of the raft and row from the rear. If you see a plane overhead, wave, holler, and generally act like a goof. Trust me: Such behavior will always attract an audience.

How to Make a Real Impact

Whether you're Chevy Chase taking a tumble to get a laugh or just an average Joe stepping on God's cosmic banana peel, going down hard won't hurt as much if you know how to cushion the blow.

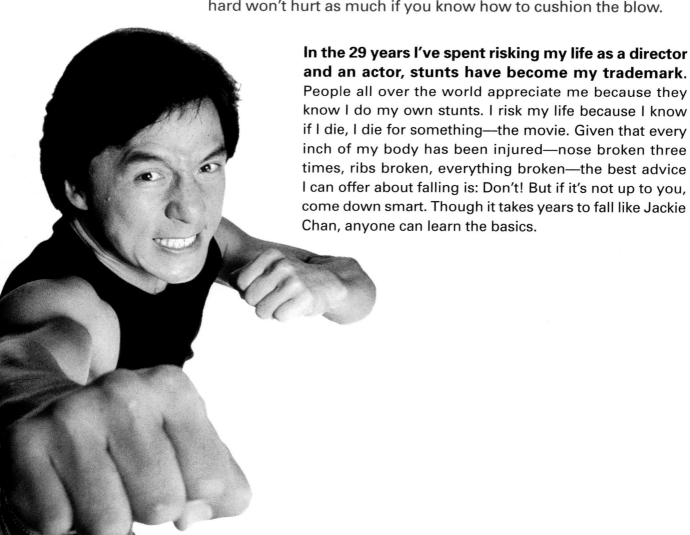

In the 29 years I've spent risking my life as a director and an actor, stunts have become my trademark. People all over the world appreciate me because they know I do my own stunts. I risk my life because I know if I die, I die for something—the movie. Given that every inch of my body has been injured—nose broken three times, ribs broken, everything broken—the best advice I can offer about falling is: Don't! But if it's not up to you, come down smart. Though it takes years to fall like Jackie Chan, anyone can learn the basics.

1 FALL INTO POSITION

Hit the ground safely.

When most people fall, they're stiff as board or limp as rag doll. Prepare your body for impact. You need to protect your head and back most of all. And it's much better to land on your shoulders, thighs, and feet (see arrows) than your hands, which contain many little bones. If you must use your arms, use them to prevent impact with your face. If you land on your groin or face, you won't go to the next step. You'll go to the hospital. If you feel scared and want to release tension, do what I do: Scream. I start every jump with "Ahhhhh!"

2 DON'T LAND ON YOUR HEAD

Be very careful not to fall on your head.

When I was shooting *The Armor of God* in Yugoslavia, I almost died. I jumped from a castle to a tree, and the tree broke. I kept falling— 25 feet in all. I thought I was safe because I aimed for a Yugoslavian cameraman. I figured he'd break my fall, but he picked up the camera and ran! Instead of hitting heads with a Serb, my skull hit a rock, and now I have a hole in the top of my head. Not everybody has as hard a head as Jackie Chan. So don't go face-to-face with Mother Earth. Believe me, two broken legs are better than one broken skull.

3 BE AN ACTIVE LANDER

If you fall directly on something like a rock, you'll get really hurt, but if you keep turning and rolling as you land, it's much less painful.

It can still hurt, but you probably won't die. Attack your landing. When you hit the ground, roll with it. You need to transfer the force of impact into a lot of little movements by somersaulting, turning, and tumbling. Of course, a lot depends on the height and conditions of the fall and the terrain you're hitting. Still, the basics are the same: Don't let the impact decide what happens to you next. If you think you're going to come down on a hard surface, get ready for the rock—and roll!

WILLIAM SHATNER

How to Boldly Go

In the final frontier, there are no roadside rest stops. But even in the midst of intergalactic skirmishes, nature still calls. What's a self-respecting space explorer to do?

As the captain of the U.S.S. *Enterprise*, I've conquered a lot of new frontiers. One of the big downsides, though, is that when you're exploring a planet for hours on end, you can occasionally find yourself in lower-G.I. distress. No matter how far out in space you've gone, how desolate the planet, or how hostile its occupants, when you have to go, you have to go. It can be an issue, really. And, to be frank, even on *Star Trek,* you can't just beam yourself back up to the *Enterprise* during these times. Scotty gets pretty peeved, and the rest of the crew complains. I hate it when they yell, "Shatner!" and throw the Airwick across the bridge. That's why every now and then, you have to stop what you're doing and boldly go where no man has gone before.

1 STEER CLEAR OF INTELLIGENT LIFE

As you're exploring the far reaches of the universe, you need to be mindful of environmental impact.

What you leave behind today can end up in the water supply of some unsuspecting life form tomorrow. As a rule, make sure that you're on high ground and at least 150 feet from water sources. Also, make sure that you're well off the beaten path. This is exactly when you don't want to seek out new civilizations.

2 TAKE THE RIGHT TECHNOLOGY

Wherever it is you're boldly going, take time to do a little excavation.

You should disturb the surface of the planet as little as possible. So make sure your captain's log, and any other evidence of your presence, is well hidden. There's no need to tunnel to the planet's core. The organisms you want to reach—those involved in decomposition—are in the first 6 to 8 inches of topsoil. In warmer climates, you can clear a site in less than a minute. In areas with subzero temperatures or deep snow, dig until you reach earth.

3 KNOW THE ENEMY

As I've learned on many occasions, even when the native environment looks hospitable, insidious villains may be lurking all around you.

So as you're completing your mission, check for potentially hostile flora and fauna (see below). The primary objective is to make a clean getaway. If you are caught with your pants down and the wrong life form is massed at your flanks, you'll be one miserable customer down at sick bay.

GORN

POISON OAK

KLINGON

POISON IVY

TRIBBLE

POISON SUMAC

How to Deliver a Punch

It comes out of nowhere. Suddenly you're reeling without feeling. That's jake: After all, what good's a punch if you don't feel it?

It's hard to make friends in the world of boxing. There are essentially three kinds of people: those who are trying to beat you senseless, those who are betting that you're going to get beaten senseless, and those who are threatening to come out of retirement any day and beat you senseless. It's not a tranquil life. So when me and my sparring partners get together for a few rounds, we spend most of the time talking punch talk. Check out these bowl-and-ladle tips. Drink 'em in. By paying attention, anybody can become a contender.

1 PACK POWER IN THE PUNCH

If you want to get your guests firmly in your corner, give them a punch that's going to whack them in the mug.

There are dozens of different combinations you can throw at them, but here's a simple one for summer: Take a 6-ounce can of frozen lemon juice, empty it into a pitcher, and stir in ⅔ cup of light corn syrup. When you're ready to serve up the concoction, pour in a quart of ginger ale and mix. Personally, I don't drink, so that's enough for me. But what you decide to serve in the form of alcohol is up to you. You can go all the way from the equivalent of a tap on the head to a real knockout punch. Pacing is important, though, so figure no more than an ounce and a half of alcohol per person, per hour.

2 DELIVER IT RIGHT

For a punch to be properly delivered, presentation is everything. If you don't have a punch bowl, try a Crock-Pot, a baseball helmet, a cooler, a baby pool, or a wheelbarrow.

Cool it with a big block of ice—those dinky ice cubes will only melt and weaken your punch. How to make a block of ice: Fill a milk carton with water, then figure out what to do next. If you just can't work it out, you should duck the punch, because it won't make you smarter. (For a hint, see the illustration below.) If you want to, throw in some lemon, lime, or orange slices, mint sprigs, berries, or whatever you've got lying around. If you're making two punches, one with and one without alcohol, you'll be able to tell them apart, since the ice will melt much faster in the spiked version.

3 KNOW WHEN TO COUNT 'EM OUT

Some people just don't know how to handle a punch.

One minute they're animated and on their toes; the next they're making sloppy passes at every heavy bag in the room. Technically,

this is what's known as "punch drunk." Before you let anybody go another round, wave two fingers in front of his face and see if he can track the movement with his eyes. If he has trouble, it's time to throw in the towel and make up the couch.

TONY RANDALL

How to Plant a Seed in Autumn

A guy becomes a father for the first time when he hits 77. What does he learn from that? How to plan for pumpkins, of course.

Sowing is a springtime thing. But I say, long live autumn. A couple of years ago, Jack Klugman and I enlivened the venerable Haymarket Theater in London in a summer production of *The Odd Couple.* It's an exhausting play, but still my Sundays were free. Most Sundays, I went to Glyndebourne for the opera. But not every Sunday. I've learned that when you take up planting, even in autumn, you can still harvest something beautiful. All you really need is enough love and attention to nurture what you've planted so it can grow strong.

1 FIND FERTILE GROUND

When you're planting in spring, you can raise anything. But if, like me, you wait until September, your growing season is short. That's why I prefer to grow baby pumpkins. They mature in just a few months, and you can grow them indoors in a large container and up a trellis. To begin with, make sure you're dealing with fecund ground. Here's my fertility test: Pour a bucket of water on the spot where you plan to sow. Wait 5 minutes, then take a look: If there's any water pooling on the surface, your seed won't stand much of a chance. Look instead for a location with good drainage.

2 MASTER THE TECHNIQUE

Get in there with a good garden tool. Loosen the soil [A]. Now, here's an insider tip: Moisten the ground [B] before you plant the seed [C]. That way it'll stay exactly where you planted it. Water after planting, and the seed will move around and you won't know exactly what you'll get—unless you have a sonogram machine at home, I suppose.

3 KNOW WHAT YOUR PUMPKIN WILL LOOK LIKE

All baby plants look somewhat alike, so you want to be able to pick your pumpkin out of a crowd—especially if the crowd is filled with undesirables that you'll want to weed out. So if you're planting in a garden, save a couple of the seeds and plant them in a pot with a combination of one-third peat, one-third vermiculite, and one-third compost. Then put the pot in a sunny window. As your seedlings emerge, you'll be able to tell what the pumpkin in the garden

should look like by comparing it to what's in the pot. This is a good trick for making sure that you don't yank the vine, thinking it's the product of a bad seed. Keep watering, keep nurturing, and remember: It's never too late to sow.

GARRY KASPAROV

How to Pull the Plug on a Computer

Your old computer finally beat? Ready to toss it on the trash heap of office-equipment history? Don't make any rash moves or get rooked by technology. Here's what you need to know first.

Who said technology was going to make life better? Must've been Lenin or Gates, because all technology has done is make more work for the masses—while it makes more money for the capitalists. Technology hasn't shortened the workweek; it's brought it home for the weekend. Now nobody has time for smarter diversions, like board games. Instead, cell phones are ringing, fax machines are spewing paper, and e-mails are piling up faster than you can say, "Put down that bottle, Boris!" And don't even get me started on computers. They're a real rook. After all, a bunch of know-it-alls said that these would make people obsolete, but they really don't. They just make other, older computers obsolete. And this leaves a question: Once you've used and abused your computer, beaten the bytes out of it, how do you put all that artificial intelligence out of its misery?

1 BE A BYTE KNIGHT

If your PC is still in good working order, the best idea is to donate it to a nonprofit organization or school.

You can find a list of places looking for donated computers by signing onto this Web site: www.libertynet.org/share. Not only will you land yourself a hefty tax write-off, but it's also good for your public image. If your computer is one of the early Mac models, there's a growing number of collectors who'd like to talk to you. You can find them online or in the classifieds in the back of Mac magazines.

2 PAWN IT

The best thing about a brain-dead computer? No organ-donor-card hassles.

Just open the case and remove the most valuable parts (inset), which are usually the hard drive, CD-ROM, memory chips or cards, and video cards. (These typically aren't what made your computer act up anyway.) Sell these to a local parts dealer, then check the yellow pages for a local recycling company that can take the computer off your hands. Even if your computer's fine and it's just that your favorite applications are defeating you, call the recycler anyway! Your local recycler is the ultimate Alt+F4.

3 KEEP YOUR TEMPER IN CHECK, MATE

If there's nothing useful left in your PC, you can't just smash it into smithereens and leave it out on the street, even if it's annoying the hell out of you.

You must play by the rules. Computers are insidious machines loaded with toxic waste. For example, the monitor contains things like lead and radioactive materials. And I've heard that some computers even have viruses! That's why throwing a computer out a window (no matter which version you have handy) isn't an option—even though you may think the exercise will help you overcome the deep blues.

How to Do Your Part to Win

Football is a lot like growing hair—it's a constant battle for control of the turf. You win some—and then suddenly you lose a lot. Time to make a few tough choices. Do you go long, or play for short yardage?

You wonder what a winning quarterback is carrying inside that helmet? The whole game, that's what. But sometimes that's all: Believe me, when you sit in the press box every week watching quarterbacks pull off their helmets, you see a whole lot of blown coverages. Nevertheless, one thing I've learned about football is that sometimes the best plays come right off the top of your head. A single brush with inspiration can make up for 59 minutes of harebrained plays. So take it from an old quarterback: When you get sacked behind the hairline, call a play that'll help recover lost yardage. Here's the whole-pate playbook, the key strategies that will help you win back the control you need—along with a few other bonehead plays that will make sure you'll never have enough coverage to win.

1 THE WINNERS

Off-center formation:
Find the point above the left eyebrow where the hairline recedes to its farthest point. Take the lower squad down to the ear and bring the rest up to a cross-pate lateral sweep.

Forward rush: Bring the wide receivers to the line at the last minute, creating a bigger front line. Then rush the middle forward. You'll conquer more territory than Caesar.

Punt: Sometimes you have to give up and let go of it all. If you're about to shave it away, though, be sure to keep the sidelines trimmed—or you'll look like Joe Namath without his artificial turf.

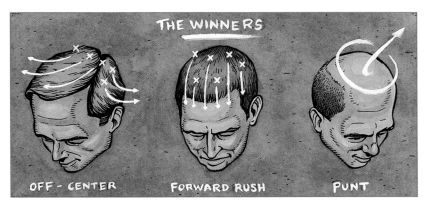

THE WINNERS

OFF-CENTER   FORWARD RUSH   PUNT

2 THE LOSERS

Lateral sweep: Start low on the field, move slightly forward, then cut wide across the forehead to intercept the opposite-noggin fringe.

Split T: Start high on the crown, fall down in two equal patterns, then make a slight feint forward, ending the play with a backfield sweep above the ears.

The bomb: Here, the whole front line drops back to form a pocket, while you hope no one spots the uncovered man. It's a hail-Mary toss at best.

THE LOSERS

LATERAL SWEEP   SPLIT T   THE BOMB

TOM JONES

How to Pick Up Lingerie

Thoughtful guys ask, "What kind of gift just keeps on giving?" You want something that's sweet. Something that says you care. Something that shouts, "You're my lady!" So how about crotchless panties?

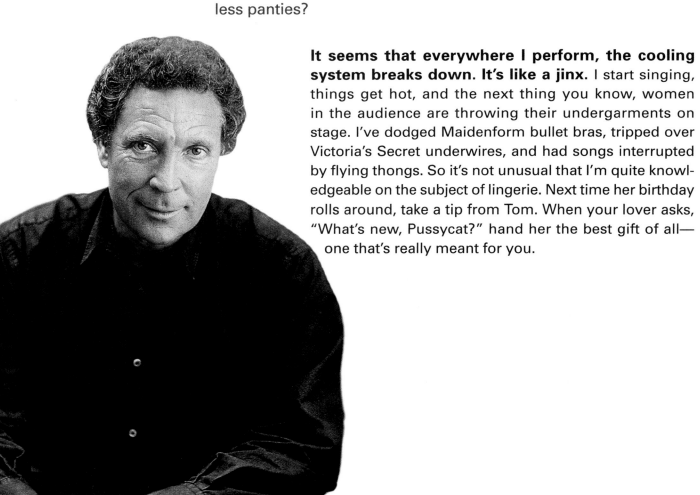

It seems that everywhere I perform, the cooling system breaks down. It's like a jinx. I start singing, things get hot, and the next thing you know, women in the audience are throwing their undergarments on stage. I've dodged Maidenform bullet bras, tripped over Victoria's Secret underwires, and had songs interrupted by flying thongs. So it's not unusual that I'm quite knowledgeable on the subject of lingerie. Next time her birthday rolls around, take a tip from Tom. When your lover asks, "What's new, Pussycat?" hand her the best gift of all—one that's really meant for you.

1 SIZING HER UP

First you need to know her bra size.

A bra is a serious piece of engineering. If the bra is too small, the wires that offer support may cut into breast tissue and hurt; too big, and the bra looks unattractive and wrinkled. The proper bra will fit comfortably and make her feel like a lady. The stress points are on the shoulders and the area just below the puppies, where an underwire can dig in deep. Check out some intimate items you dig on her and look at their labels. For a bra, the tag is usually near the hooks, sewn into a seam. Unfortunately, a lot of women find labels irritating and cut them off. If this is the case, simply steal off to the store with the garment. Nothing commands the attention of a sullen salesgirl like a guy taking his girlfriend's camisole out for a walk.

2 CHECK OUT THE HARDWARE

The type of body your girl has should dictate the kind of lingerie you're going to buy for her.

- ◾ A baby-doll nightie that comes down to just above the knee is good for all shapes.
- ◾ A bustier may be too much for a well-endowed woman: There's no need to gild the lily.
- ◾ A teddy is very difficult for most women to wear. If the woman in your life can audition to become a Spice Girl, go for it. Otherwise, buy one at your own risk, or seek out some of the newer ones that are made with stretchier laces and form-fitting microfibers.
- ◾ Any woman looks good in a garter belt and stockings; they really show off her stems. But will she wear them? They tend to be uncomfortable for everyday use, so I recommend them for show time only.

BABY-DOLL   BUSTIER

TEDDY   GARTER BELT

3 GET IN TOUCH WITH HER FEMININE SIDE

Once you've made your choice, start thinking about what comes next.

The word most women use for this kind of conceptualizing is *accessories.* So if you've decided to get her a bustier, go the rest of the way and pick up a pair of 5-inch heels. If a garter belt's your choice, go for the thong. If your preference is a teddy, drop some coin on some diamond earrings. In other words, if you're going to go for a hit, go for the homer. If you know your woman well, there's no chance of striking out.

MANUEL A. NORIEGA

How to Become a Strongman

A man. A plan. A confined space. A workout.

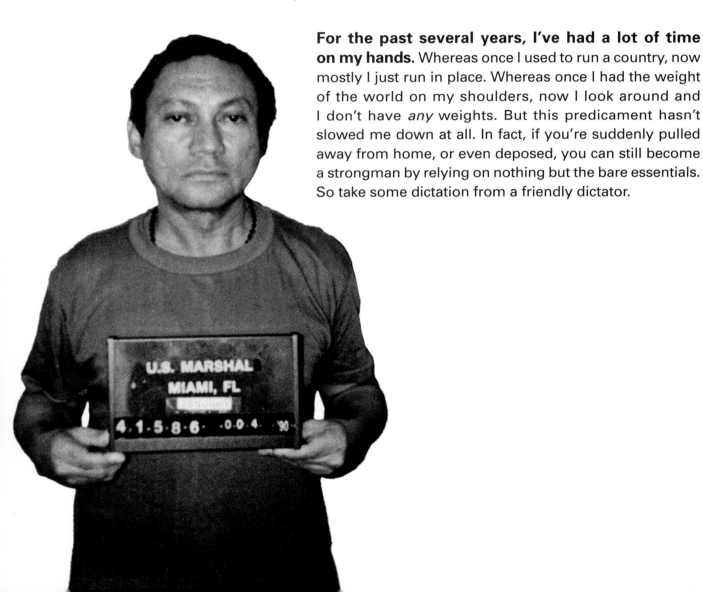

For the past several years, I've had a lot of time on my hands. Whereas once I used to run a country, now mostly I just run in place. Whereas once I had the weight of the world on my shoulders, now I look around and I don't have *any* weights. But this predicament hasn't slowed me down at all. In fact, if you're suddenly pulled away from home, or even deposed, you can still become a strongman by relying on nothing but the bare essentials. So take some dictation from a friendly dictator.

1 THE PUSHUP

This is an old standby that doesn't require much room and will work your chest, shoulders, and arms.

Lie facedown on the floor with your feet together and your hands shoulder-width apart. Then push yourself up until your arms are fully extended. Keep your back straight, and do as many as you can. If, like me, you find that maintaining power is extra important, mount a greater resistance by placing your feet on a bunk. It increases the angle and makes the exercise tougher.

2 THE SITUP

To be an effective strongman, you need to have a strong stomach.

So do this: Lie on your back with your knees bent and the bottoms of your legs up on a chair. Cross your hands over your chest. Now curl up until your shoulder blades are 4 to 6 inches off the floor. Keep your eyes focused on the wall above your knees. Hold the position for a second before lowering your shoulders to the floor.

3 THE CHAIR DIP

This exercise is essential if you're focused on a great arms buildup.

With your feet together and resting on top of a bunk, place your hands, with your palms facing each other, on the edges of a chair that's a couple of inches behind your butt. Slowly lower yourself until your upper arms are parallel to the floor, then push yourself back up until your arms are extended. If you're lucky enough to have some bars in your window, end the workout with a set of pullups. It's a great way to finish out your regime.

WERNER KLEMPERER

How to Be a Happy Camper

You can tell the losers from the winners in any war by figuring out this: who has to go camping and who wants to go camping. If Mother Nature is your commandant, you'd better learn to follow orders.

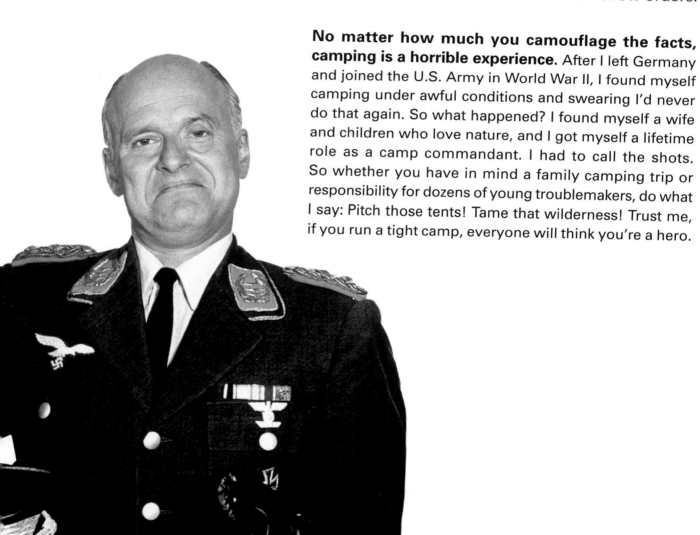

No matter how much you camouflage the facts, camping is a horrible experience. After I left Germany and joined the U.S. Army in World War II, I found myself camping under awful conditions and swearing I'd never do that again. So what happened? I found myself a wife and children who love nature, and I got myself a lifetime role as a camp commandant. I had to call the shots. So whether you have in mind a family camping trip or responsibility for dozens of young troublemakers, do what I say: Pitch those tents! Tame that wilderness! Trust me, if you run a tight camp, everyone will think you're a hero.

1 ORGANIZE YOUR CAMP

You must have the commanding view. So search for an established campsite on high ground; you'll find fresher air and meet up with fewer vermin.

Stay at least 200 feet away from lakes or streams and 2 miles from a major road, town, or ammunition depot. In the center of camp, use an existing fire pit and pitch your tent on level soil upwind of it. Instruct your troops that the "latrine" is a stretch of forest downhill from your campsite and 150 feet away from any water source. And show them how to dig—and refill—8-inch-deep "cat holes." Last, remember to hang all your food 10 feet up and well out on a limb, so the animals can't reach it. This makes retrieving food tedious. Anyone misbehaves, he gets the cooler.

2 MAINTAIN CAMP DISCIPLINE

Camping should be a serene experience without the distraction of rock 'n' roll or news broadcasts.

The sounds you hear should be those made by your hard-working charges and the birds. In the night, you may find yourself awakened by some disturbance amongst the tents. Of course, when you investigate, nobody knows anything! They feign innocence! But you know better! You know somebody is lying! Who? Who? You must make them talk! To do this, just take away their Walkmans.

3 POST ORDERS

Nature is a complete shambles.

Dirt is everywhere, and there is no order to the rocks and trees and such. So make every man do his part by posting a duty sheet outlining everyone's jobs. Assign someone to firewood detail, KP, cleanup—whatever.

Once the group is a well-oiled machine, the camp will run with the breathtaking efficiency of a Mercedes burning 93. Remember: It's Man against Nature. Camping is war, and war, as you know, is hell.

DON KING

How to Train a Boxer

He's just a rough, raw pup from the streets, but you can see that he has what it takes to be a champion. All he needs is a little instruction in the manly arts.

I may be the biggest, baddest, best promoter of all time, but I didn't achieve that all alone. I did it by hooking up with the strongest, smartest, best-trained boxers in the world. That last part's key—good training always beats speed and brawn. Now, I preach the basics; some promoters like to put on a nice little dog-and-pony show at training camp, but who needs a boxer who dances around in the air like a whirligig? Uh-uh. I say, start with the simple stuff, and you'll have your boxer sitting pretty in no time.

1 OFFER THE RIGHT PRIZE

First, remember that boxers are just like people: They want the good things in life, and they're willing to fight to get them.

What you need to do is match the reward to the boxer. Muhammad Ali, he wanted respect and a chance to speak his mind. George Foreman, he wants people to like him and not hassle him about burgers. Some boxers are easier than that. Some boxers you can motivate with nothing more than an old ham bone.

2 DON'T TRY TO PUSH YOUR ADVANTAGE

Look, all boxers want to be best in show, but too many times the people in their corners push them too much.

No boxer responds to having somebody ride his butt all day. And whatever you do, don't look a boxer in the eye. In his teeny, tiny little brainpan, a boxer sees that as a challenge.

3 PUT HIM ON THE CANVAS

To get your boxer to sit up and take notice of your commands, do this:

Start about 3 feet in front of the standing dog. Hold a ham bone so he has to look up to see it. Once you have his attention, take one step toward him as you move the bone up toward your chest. To keep the bone in sight, the dog will lower his butt. Once he's down, say "Sit!" and throw him the bone. You've just taught this boxer a lesson. A little more training and your boxer will be all over the newspapers—guaranteed!

NO BEGGING LICKING

How to Make the Greens

Want a course that's guaranteed to give you the edge?

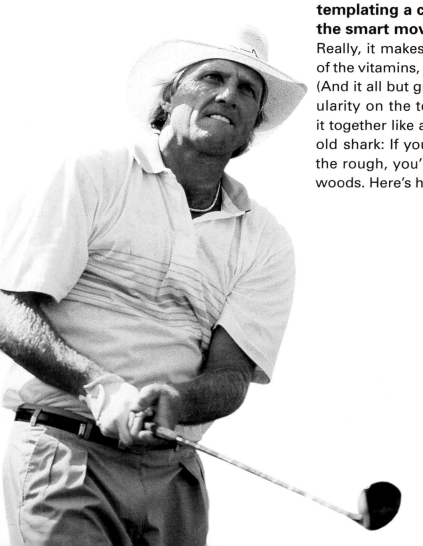

Recently I was puttering around the kitchen, contemplating a chip or two, when I decided that, hey, the smart move would be to just go for the greens. Really, it makes sense. A good salad caddies almost all of the vitamins, minerals, and fiber an athlete could want. (And it all but guarantees to provide you with some regularity on the tour.) All you need is a fair way to bring it together like a master. So follow some advice from an old shark: If you stay the course with a watchful eye to the rough, you'll be able to keep your health out of the woods. Here's how to make the most of your salad days.

1 MASTER THE DRIVE

You want to make a statement right from the opening shot.

So use your head. Step up, hold the lettuce in your hand, and bring it back in a smooth, even stroke [A]. A good backswing provides the strength you need for what comes next: the drive. Bring the head forward swiftly, but don't muscle it with your shoulders. Instead, let the rotation of your hips bring the stem end of the head firmly into contact with the counter [B]. If your aim is good, you'll bust it right down the middle. Now twist out the core. Among your heads of lettuce, you now have a hole in one.

2 AVOID SAND TRAPS AND WATER HAZARDS

Sometimes greens can be gritty, especially if you haven't properly watered them.

On the other hand, you don't want greens that are sopping wet. So after you rinse them, take 'em for a spin. Spin counterclockwise [C]. Stop. Dump out the excess water [D]. Then spin 'em clockwise [E]. Now you've got majestic greens you can play with.

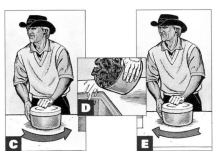

3 DRESS RIGHT

When a man has his own clothing line, he can't be seen strolling the links with some fatty, heavy blue-cheese dressing smeared on his golf shirt.

So dress your salad right: Use tomatoes, peppers, grated carrots, and onion or garlic. This ups the fiber content of your meal—and this is one time it's okay to be in the rough. Next, coat the greens with a nice low-fat dressing: Take 2 tablespoons of Dijon mustard, 1 of honey, and a splash each of lemon and orange juice, and mix. Then pour it on top. I guarantee it'll bring your game up to par and make you a pro around the greens in no time.

CHARLTON HESTON

How to Let Your People Go

Sometimes you have to deliver a message from on high, and sometimes that message ain't pretty. So take it from a guy who played Moses—and knows a thing or two about sacrificial lambs.

I've got a reputation as a bit of a tough guy, and for good reason: I have raced chariots, faced down pharaohs, even been held captive by apes (which, whenever I sit through congressional gun-control hearings, sparks an odd sense of déjà vu). But even tough guys have a hard time setting their people free, whether it means parting the Red Sea or issuing a pink slip. When the time for goodbyes is at hand, you need to be strong. Don't bequeath this role to an underling: If you're the one who giveth, you're the one who must taketh away. To help your people make that great journey into a new and better life, I beseech you to follow these three commandments.

1 FIRST COMMANDMENT: THOU SHALT GATHER THY PEOPLE AROUND YOU

When someone's setting out for a new land—even if it's against his will—it's important for him to have allies to see him off.

So before you come down from the mountain to deliver a disciple from corporate slavery and send him on his flight to a new homeland, recruit

someone the employee likes and respects to stand beside you and help soften the blow. And don't pick someone who will benefit from the firing. That's breaking the 11th commandment: Thou shalt not covet thy neighbor's cubicle.

2 SECOND COMMANDMENT: THOU SHALT EMPOWER THY PEOPLE

Prepare something in writing— a personnel file, a memo, a stone tablet—telling them exactly why they're being set free.

Then, give them a choice: Do they want to receive a sermon from the mount or read the word themselves? It may not seem like an important step, but your mission is to give them the feeling that they have some modicum of control. After all, they're going forth armed with nothing but faith and a curriculum vitae.

3 THIRD COMMANDMENT: THOU SHALT SET THEM FREE

Once you've pushed your people out on their holy quest, let them find their own way.

Too often, leaders feel the need to shepherd their people for too long, and the next thing they know, they've turned the Promised Land into a welfare state. That's a mistake of biblical proportions. Take heed: Better a plague of locusts than a plague of former employees trolling your kingdom for handouts.

KEN GRIFFEY JR.

How to Be Safe at Home

In baseball, the whole object is to get home. But what if you get home and nothing's there? Then you realize that to a crook, home is where the score is.

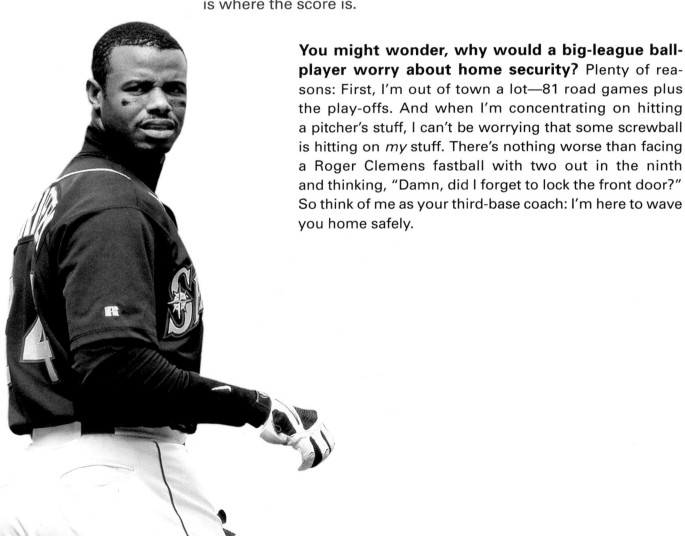

You might wonder, why would a big-league ballplayer worry about home security? Plenty of reasons: First, I'm out of town a lot—81 road games plus the play-offs. And when I'm concentrating on hitting a pitcher's stuff, I can't be worrying that some screwball is hitting on *my* stuff. There's nothing worse than facing a Roger Clemens fastball with two out in the ninth and thinking, "Damn, did I forget to lock the front door?" So think of me as your third-base coach: I'm here to wave you home safely.

1 DRILL ONE DOWN THE FOUL LINE

As a kid, I broke plenty of windows bashing baseballs, so I know how easy it is to get past the glass.

If you're worried about something bigger than a baseball breaking in, try this: Drill a hole on the left and right sides of the inside frame, 6 inches above where the top and bottom sashes meet. Then insert a nail in each hole. Now, even if somebody breaks the window and unlocks the latch, it'll be harder to open the window. Of course, you're smart enough not to make the nails too snug; in case of fire, you need to make an easy out.

2 GET OUT OF THE BUSH LEAGUES

I like to steal a base or two from time to time, and I can tell you that theft is a crime of opportunity.

You wait until your opponent is distracted, then you take off. So don't give a thief a big lead! One of the stupidest things you can do is put nice, decorative, easy-to-hide-behind hedges all around your house. It's like throwing a burglar a hanging curve. If you've got a green thumb, plant holly shrubs [A] and roses [B]. They're sharper than a Pedro Martinez slider.

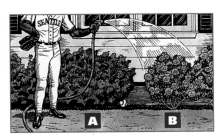

3 LIGHT THE FIELD

Look, if I played for the Cubs, I'd tell you that electric light is a no-no.

But the more wattage around your cottage, the better. And you can make your field of dreams even less appealing if it's guarded well by your designated hitter. My recommendation: Get yourself a big, ugly dog.

ALEX TREBEK

How to Pop the Question

To live life just before prime time, you have to be prepared, read your clues, and phrase your request in just the right way.

After 15 years as host of *Jeopardy!*, I've learned an important lesson: It's better to be the guy with all the answers than the guy with all the questions. Even if you think you know what the answer's going to be, you can still lose big by phrasing the question incorrectly. So if you've been scanning the game board of life and you think you've found a category you can sweep off its feet, take some advice from a seasoned quizmaster. Here's how to make a strategic wager and take home that prized partner.

1 JEOPARDY

Before you take the stage, you have to know this: If she's the right answer, what precisely is the question?

If your question is "Who is the last woman I'll ever make love to?" and you're fine with the answer, great. Proceed to the next challenge. But if your question is "Who is a convenient solution to my bachelorhood problem?" then heed my advice and don't ring in yet! Guys who think they've found an answer when they don't even know the important questions will end up forfeiting half of all their cash and prizes.

2 DOUBLE JEOPARDY

When you've selected "Precious Gems for $3,000," be sure to fine-tune your negotiating skills.

No price is set in stone. You might be able to strike a deal for up to 20 percent off advertised prices. Best time to bargain: August (after the big wedding season) or just after Christmas. But pay attention, contestants. Look for a diamond that's bright and sparkly. Bright and sparkly means you're playing in the Tournament of Champions. Dull and cloudy means you're taking home the consolation prize.

3 FINAL JEOPARDY

Some guys whisk their woman off to Paris, others slip a ring into a fortune cookie, and still others just mutter, "So, you wanna get hitched or what?" during the seventh-inning stretch.

Whatever your courting style, keep in mind: This is the round that will play in her mental reruns forever. Eye contact tells her you're serious.

A bent knee represents respect for her. Now, pop the question. If she says, "You're the new champion," congratulations! (Be sure to shake hands politely with the runners-up.) And remember: No more calling up your old friend Vanna for another free spin. You're playing lifetime *Jeopardy!* now.

How Not to Be Left

Look! Up in the air! It's a bird! No! It's your plane! Maybe you've just run out of time, out of ideas, and out of luck.

Being a congressman is tough work. It's not enough just to be right; you also have to make sure you're not caught behind the times. Take me, for example: When I'd stake out a position on a balanced budget and tax cuts, a lot of people would follow my lead. So I had to be there first. And it's the same when I travel. Perfect timing is crucial. But those who have a more liberal approach to travel schedules? Well, they're the misguided ones who are nearly always left at the gate.

1 PACK CONSERVATIVELY

The first rule of not being left: Travel light. Cut heavy layers of wasteful carpetbags.

If you limit yourself to just one or two carry-ons of the proper dimensions, there's no chance of a veto down the line. And no matter what some people promise at election time, extra luggage in the overhead bin is not an entitlement.

RIGHT

WRONG

2 CHECK THE RECORDS

You wouldn't vote for a candidate without checking his record on tax hikes, would you?

Well, when you're planning a connecting flight, you can check your flight's performance record, too. See, the airlines assign every flight an on-time performance rating from 1 to 9. One means the flight arrives on schedule 10 percent of the time; 9 means nearly 100 percent. The airlines won't volunteer that information, though. You'll have to ask the

ticket agent, "What is your on-time performance rating?" If they don't measure up, don't elect to fly with them again.

3 MAKE YOUR OWN CALL

As a Republican, I sometimes make liberals angry because they think I occasionally step out of line.

But a guy who doesn't want to be left must stand up and say what's right. So if you have reservations for a flight and you find yourself

mysteriously bumped off, don't wait at the ticket counter looking for a handout. By the time you reach the desk, every alternate flight will be booked—and you may end up in D.C. as a punishment. Instead, call the airline's 800 number directly. They'll set you up right—so you'll never again have to worry about being left.

How to Test-Drive a Used Car

Attention, car shoppers: Sometimes you can spot a winner with just a simple lap around the block. The trick is knowing what to look for once you're in the driver's seat.

I've spent a lot of years testing the limits of cars, seeing what they can do and then making them do just a little bit more. But not every ride has been a smooth one. For example, my first car was actually a truck: a 1980 Chevy step-side pickup with a straight six, a three-speed on the column, and no power steering. I was 16, and I'd earned my license in a driver's-ed car with an automatic, so I didn't know what that other pedal down there was for. I just put it in "3," hoped for the best, and drove my truck all the way home. I spent the next 6 months rebuilding it, repainting it, putting on new wheels and tires, and generally trying to make it look like I'd known what I was doing when I bought it. In a decade of driving one car after another since then, this is what I've come to look for the first time around.

1 LISTEN TO THE MUSIC
What do you want to hear when you start a car?

As little as possible. The engine should hum along smoothly; if you hear a chorus of pings, clicks, whines, and other odd noises, you're listening to a lemon. Also take time to have a look at all the maintenance records. That means all of them, not just the bill for the rebuilt engine or the new rear axle. And keep in mind that the signs of a bad car are usually small signs, so look the whole thing over closely for quick repairs, painted-over rust spots, and evidence of accidents.

2 DRIVE STRAIGHT; TURN LEFT
Is it an automatic?

Drop it down into "drive" and see how it handles the pull. The transition should be tight and seamless. A manual transmission helps you evaluate the car's performance: The more gears it has, the better you'll be able to judge its muscle and capabilities. As you approach that left turn, you want steering sensitive enough to let you feel the ground under the tires, but not so sensitive that you have to work to turn the car. A sloppy suspension and flabby steering are dangerous, but steering that's too tight will wear you out just trying to parallel park. The real test-drive begins when you pull out onto the highway. Open it up. You should hear a deep, satisfying roar. Acceleration should be smooth and effortless.

3 THE PITS
No matter how well your car runs when you take it out for a spin, you're going to be very disappointed if it doesn't stop.

Take the car from cruising speed to a full stop in as short a distance as possible without skidding. The car should brake in a straight line, without pulling to either side. We can't use antilock brakes in NASCAR Winston Cup Racing, but they're a must anywhere else. Test-driving a car with bad brakes? Look for one of two things: a different car or a lot of trouble at the end of the road.

How to Clean Out the Gutter

There are some things no right-minded guy wants hanging over his head. A pile of sludge is one.

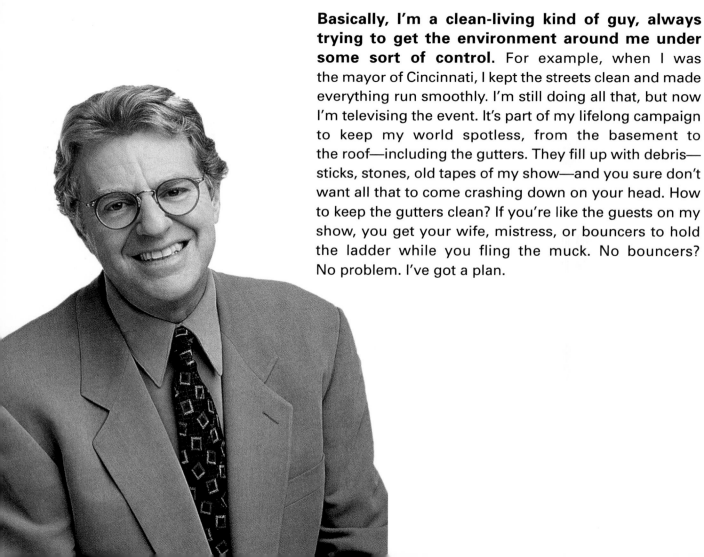

Basically, I'm a clean-living kind of guy, always trying to get the environment around me under some sort of control. For example, when I was the mayor of Cincinnati, I kept the streets clean and made everything run smoothly. I'm still doing all that, but now I'm televising the event. It's part of my lifelong campaign to keep my world spotless, from the basement to the roof—including the gutters. They fill up with debris—sticks, stones, old tapes of my show—and you sure don't want all that to come crashing down on your head. How to keep the gutters clean? If you're like the guests on my show, you get your wife, mistress, or bouncers to hold the ladder while you fling the muck. No bouncers? No problem. I've got a plan.

1 TAKE THE HIGH GROUND

Ever since I started beating Oprah in the ratings, I've been aware of how dangerous it is to be on top.

My advice to those who climb: Observe the rule of 4:1. If your ladder is 12 feet high, the base should be 3 feet from the house. Any farther and your insurance rating plummets, along with you and the ladder.

2 RAID HER DRAWERS

You'll be surprised what useful stuff you can find if you rummage through your wife's implements.

For example, that spatula she uses to flip pancakes is just the tool you need to scrape the muck out of the gutters. It's all in the leverage. Just send the spatula through the dishwasher before Sunday brunch.

3 HOSE 'EM DOWN

Sometimes you just have to clear the set.

After you've removed the leaves, flush the system: Push the nozzle of a hose into the downspout and crank up the pressure full blast. When the trash shoots out the bottom, you're clear.

4 SCREEN CAREFULLY AGAINST UNWANTED SCUM

One lesson I've learned from show biz: You can't screen too carefully, especially when you're dealing with debris.

So after you've completed the cleaning process, save yourself a lot of work by installing plastic or aluminum gutter screens to keep the crud from piling up. You'll find them in the hardware store. That should prevent further clogs and leave your afternoons free for daytime TV. One last thing: If your gutters are more than 20 feet high, hire a pro. Just make sure your check clears.

ROGER MOORE

How to Make a Perfect Bond

In a world where double crosses and double agents can make things fall apart fast, it pays to know how to put them back together.

Playing Secret Agent 007 had its advantages: fast cars, nifty gadgets, cummerbunds. But there's a problem with relying too much on high technology: Things fall apart. That's fine if it's a flimsy bikini, but it spells big trouble when it's something you really depend on, like a cocktail. And since I spent most of my time being chased through explosive situations by unstable women with great legs, I couldn't always rely on Q to provide the necessary fix. What's a modern secret agent to do when everything comes unglued? Reach for the glue gun and say, "Bond, James, bond."

1 TARGET THE RIGHT AGENTS

Pick the wrong agent and the bond won't last.

Just ask George Lazenby. So do it right. To glue paper, use white glue or rubber cement. To glue wood, use white glue, carpenter's glue, plastic resin glue, or construction adhesive. To glue metal, plastic, or porcelain, use epoxy or Super Glue. To glue leather, use carpenter's glue or rubber cement.

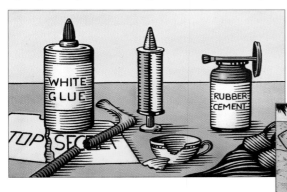

And if the broken object is the heart of a beautiful Bond girl? I wouldn't know. I'm usually in another country by then.

2 PREPARE TO MOUNT

After my very first Bond film, I learned a critical lesson about how to prevent problems with women who interfere with my duty to the Crown.

Make your break a clean one. If the surface is smooth and flat, a light sanding will do the trick. If the surface has any sort of residue, you'll need to remove it using solvent or detergent. Give the glue a good surface; just don't alter it so much that the contact zone shrinks. As I learned while grappling with Anya Amasova in *The Spy Who Loved Me,* the more contact between bare surfaces, the better.

3 FORM A SATISFYING ATTACHMENT

There are three secrets to making the bond work.

First, it's far better to cover each of the two parts with a thin, glutinous layer. Second, use restraints. (This advice works remarkably well in the bedroom, too.) A pipe-, spring-, or C-clamp will hold your parts together, if you really want to make them stick. Third, hold on until you're sure the desired results have been achieved. After all, it takes patience and skill to form a truly successful bond. When finished, I suggest you glue yourself to a vodka martini. Don't ask how to prepare it.

PETER GRAVES

How to Keep Your Tape from Self-Destructing

When you cue up the sound track for your own impossible mission, the last thing you want to hear is "pppffffft."

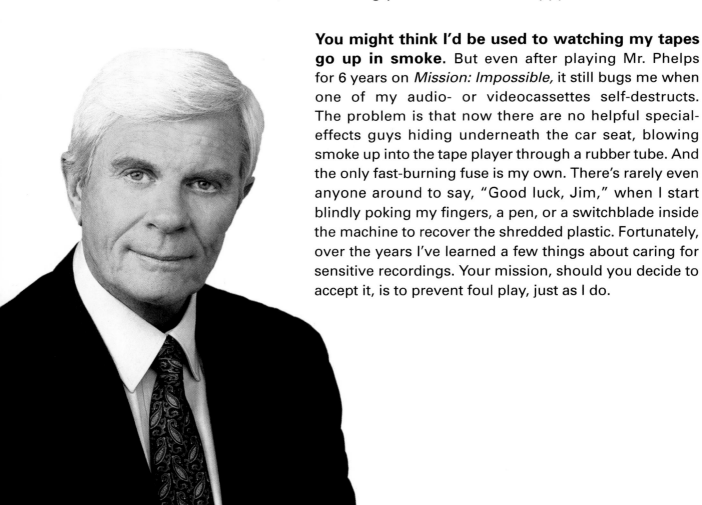

You might think I'd be used to watching my tapes go up in smoke. But even after playing Mr. Phelps for 6 years on *Mission: Impossible,* it still bugs me when one of my audio- or videocassettes self-destructs. The problem is that now there are no helpful special-effects guys hiding underneath the car seat, blowing smoke up into the tape player through a rubber tube. And the only fast-burning fuse is my own. There's rarely even anyone around to say, "Good luck, Jim," when I start blindly poking my fingers, a pen, or a switchblade inside the machine to recover the shredded plastic. Fortunately, over the years I've learned a few things about caring for sensitive recordings. Your mission, should you decide to accept it, is to prevent foul play, just as I do.

1 NEVER GET CAUGHT

Think of tapes as captives, and treat them the way you'd hope to be treated: not stashed in a car or trunk on a hot summer day.

I've been there, and it's murder on the sinuses. Give your tapes regular exercise. (A tightly wound tape, like an interrogation subject, needs to move to keep from breaking.) And store your cassettes away from moisture and direct sunlight; they last longest in a temperature around 70°F. Once your tape is damaged by heat, the quality of a great theme song can be lost forever. (Ours, by the way, was far superior to *Hawaii Five-0*'s.)

2 PROTECT AGAINST ELECTRONIC INFILTRATION

Magnetic fields can erase tapes quicker than Richard Nixon's secretary.

I've snooped around enough to know where most people keep their cassettes: audiotapes near the stereo and speakers, and videotapes on top of the TV. It's hard to imagine worse places for them. A speaker is as magnetic as Barbara Bain's lips, and a color TV automatically demagnetizes itself, so it can do the same to any treasured reruns in your collection. Other magnetic hot spots to watch out for: induction motors, like those found in refrigerators and air conditioners. So post your recordings at least 4 feet from the danger zone. Tom Cruise couldn't have told you that.

3 KEEP A CLEAR HEAD

When it comes to cleaning your cassette player, I have just one thing to say: Everclear.

It's 95 percent pure grain alcohol. Use a cotton swab to dab the tape path and heads. And keep your oily digits away from your swab and all interior parts. Don't leave any fingerprints. No telling who might be checking up on you. If you read this and still manage to screw up your tape, don't call me: I'll disavow any knowledge of you and your sorry collection of outmoded technology. Haven't you heard of CDs?

DICK CLARK

How to Preserve, Yourself

It's New Year's Eve—time to drop the big ball again. But this year, why not ring in the New Year by really jamming?

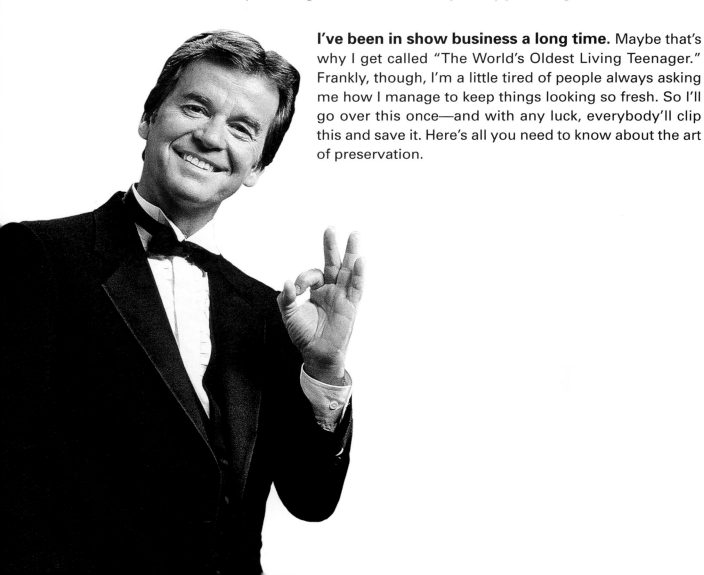

I've been in show business a long time. Maybe that's why I get called "The World's Oldest Living Teenager." Frankly, though, I'm a little tired of people always asking me how I manage to keep things looking so fresh. So I'll go over this once—and with any luck, everybody'll clip this and save it. Here's all you need to know about the art of preservation.

1. MAKE SURE YOU HAVE SOMETHING WORTH PRESERVING

Let's say you want to preserve some peaches.

Do it right: Start with something fresh and firm. You'll know a young, good-looking peach when you see one. It will have a yellowish-pink complexion and a fair amount of fuzz. What you're protecting against here are free radicals. These are the crazy molecules that cause skin to age and wrinkle, iron to rust, and fruit to turn bad. To halt their progress, grab four big peaches, scrub them clean, cut them into quarters, and remove the pits. Then toss the fruit facedown into a pan, add 3 cups of water, and simmer for 5 minutes—about the time it takes to get through a couple of verses of "Auld Lang Syne."

× 4

× 3

2. CLEANSE YOURSELF OF GERMS

To sterilize your jelly jars, fill them with plenty of water and place them apart from each other in a shallow pan partly filled with water.

Simmer the jars for 15 to 20 minutes. Meanwhile, chop your peaches into little pieces. Then toss them back into their pan along with 1 cup of sugar for each cup of fruit mixture. Add 2 ounces of pectin to thicken the preserves. Boil everything for an hour.

3. SCHEDULE REGULAR EXAMS

You never have to worry about losing freshness if you time the whole process right.

As the fruit cooks, spoon up a bit of the preserves, then let it drip back into the pan from one side of the spoon. At first, the drips will be light and syrupy. As the preserves thicken, however, two large drops will begin to form along the edge of the spoon [A]. When they come together and fall as a single large drop [B], you've reached the "sheeting stage." Time to pour your preserves into your jelly jars, screw on the lids, and get ready for the midnight celebration. Despite the passing of the New Year, your fruit will look none the worse for wear.

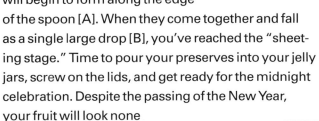

uncommon *knowledge* **57**

How to Take a Good Shot

When it's NHL season, it's flu season. Hockey fever? Hey, just surrender! But when germs come flying at you like poison pucks, you know it's time to get your flu vaccination.

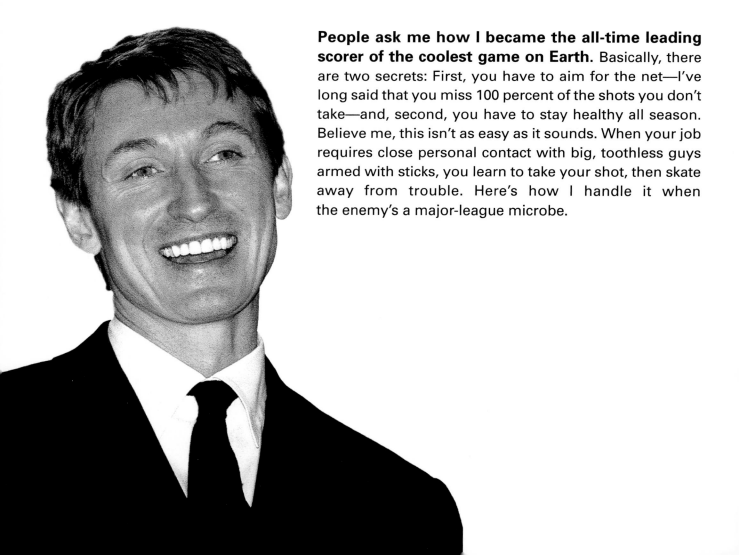

People ask me how I became the all-time leading scorer of the coolest game on Earth. Basically, there are two secrets: First, you have to aim for the net—I've long said that you miss 100 percent of the shots you don't take—and, second, you have to stay healthy all season. Believe me, this isn't as easy as it sounds. When your job requires close personal contact with big, toothless guys armed with sticks, you learn to take your shot, then skate away from trouble. Here's how I handle it when the enemy's a major-league microbe.

1 SCORE AN EARLY APPOINTMENT WITH THE TEAM DOCTOR

Hockey hurts, but night hockey really hurts, because your pain threshold is actually higher in the morning.

Fortunately, you don't have to schedule your shots around face-off times, advertisers, and fans. So if you have to take the hit, make sure you schedule it early in the day. Besides feeling less pain, you're more likely to find your doctor on schedule in the morning, meaning that you won't have to hang out in the waiting room, playing goalie to everybody else's germs.

2 GET SOME ICE TIME

When you're taking a shot, anything can happen; you have to expect the unexpected.

An angry reaction, either on the ice or on your skin, can inflict unexpected pain on your person. In this case, call up your local Zamboni operator and have him bring around some ice. This will help numb the sore area and speed your recovery time as well. But don't apply the ice directly to the skin. Wrap it in a towel first. Believe me, when you've seen as much ice time as I have, you know that a little padding makes a big difference.

3 BLOW PAST TROUBLE

I've learned from playing a lot of away games that opposing fans and players can be pretty needling, and they'll try to throw you off your game.

If someone in uniform is trying to get under your skin, there's one rule to remember: Don't tense up. To keep your cool during an important shot, take a deep breath. Your muscles are less tense when you're inhaling.

How to Build a Beach House

Tired of living in a dingy, run-down dwelling with leaky pipes and cracked linoleum? Sometimes you need to forget about this old house, repair to the beach, and build a place from scratch. Come on, it's easy.

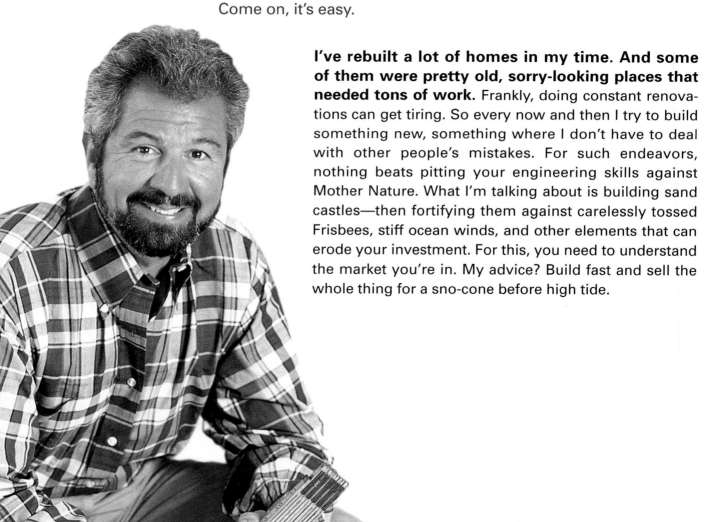

I've rebuilt a lot of homes in my time. And some of them were pretty old, sorry-looking places that needed tons of work. Frankly, doing constant renovations can get tiring. So every now and then I try to build something new, something where I don't have to deal with other people's mistakes. For such endeavors, nothing beats pitting your engineering skills against Mother Nature. What I'm talking about is building sand castles—then fortifying them against carelessly tossed Frisbees, stiff ocean winds, and other elements that can erode your investment. For this, you need to understand the market you're in. My advice? Build fast and sell the whole thing for a sno-cone before high tide.

1 THINK BIG

If you're going to create something from scratch—rather than renovating someone else's castle—you need to know how to spot a prime piece of real estate.

Scout around to find the most desirable stretch of land, preferably within 20 feet of the tide line. Farther away and the sand is too coarse and dry, and market value plunges. Scrape away the dry stuff on top

until you hit the hard layer underneath, then start thinking big. Remember, you're not building a sand hut, sand shanty, or sand trailer. You want the genuine article: an actual sand castle. So take along the materials you'll need for heavy construction: a 5-gallon bucket, a trowel, a shovel, a spray bottle, and a few different-size cups (from 8 to 32 ounces). You'll need these for constructing watchtowers to fend off marauding sand fleas.

---

2 PACK THE SAND, MAN

Take a stick and draw the castle's outline—sort of a blueprint in the sand.

Then start packing. Make a mound of sand shaped like a volcano [A]. Dump on a few gallons of water and let it sink in [B]. Then pack the sand on all sides with the shovel or a piece of board, or tamp it with a flat metal plate [C]. Keep building this way—sand, water, pack, sand, water, pack—until the desired height is reached. To make your castle last, fortify it with driftwood.

A   **B**   **C**

3 DOWNSIZE FROM THE TOP

The angle of repose for sand—that is, the point at which things begin to crumble— is about 30 degrees from horizontal.

This isn't much wiggle room. To keep the structure from collapsing under its own weight, you need to carve your castle from the top down. Maintaining balance is crucial, too. If you carve away a chunk from one side, be sure to remove an equal amount from the other. Then use seashells, pebbles, twigs, and bits of seaweed to embellish your regal establishment. And remember: If you're not happy with the results, you can always remodel.

How to Grease Your Leather

Your sweetie getting tired of a life with rawhide? Every little kiss turning into a work of friction? It might be time to soften up.

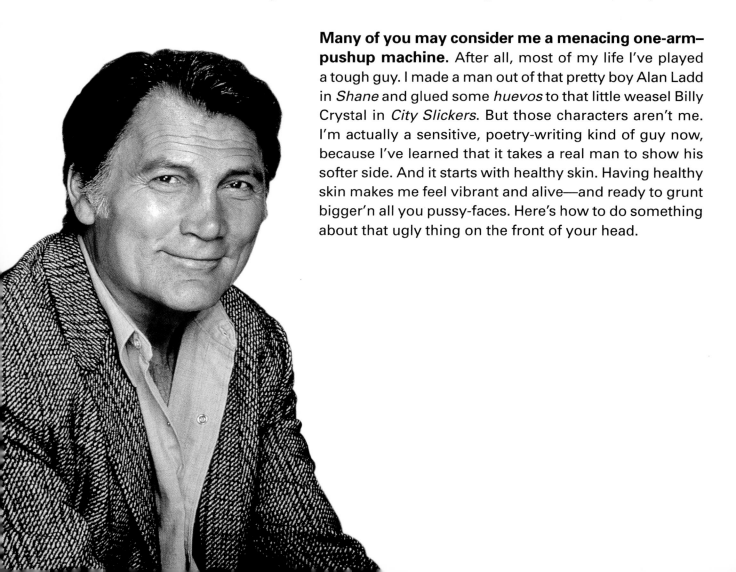

Many of you may consider me a menacing one-arm–pushup machine. After all, most of my life I've played a tough guy. I made a man out of that pretty boy Alan Ladd in *Shane* and glued some *huevos* to that little weasel Billy Crystal in *City Slickers*. But those characters aren't me. I'm actually a sensitive, poetry-writing kind of guy now, because I've learned that it takes a real man to show his softer side. And it starts with healthy skin. Having healthy skin makes me feel vibrant and alive—and ready to grunt bigger'n all you pussy-faces. Here's how to do something about that ugly thing on the front of your head.

1 GET PRETTY

There's no need to wash up with fancy name-brand creams, soaps, or lotions.

Some of that stuff's got booze in it! You'll dry that mug faster'n a south wind in Arizona. Alcohol, after all, is good for nothing except when you need a bullet removed from your behind. I like to wash with a mild, superfatted soap. Splash your face with some piss-warm water and lather up like a rabid sumbitch. Throw out that face cloth, your complexion brush, and that damn stupid polyester facial sponge—all these things are much too harsh for your skin. I use only my fingertips to wash, moving in a gentle, circular motion.

2 APPLY MOISTURIZER

I use moisturizers as often as a farmer milks a cow—twice a day.

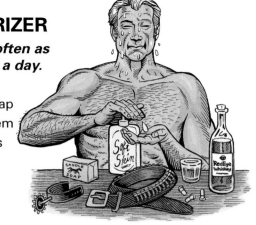

But you need to know one thing: These products are designed to trap moisture in damp skin, so slap them on when your face is wet. If there's enough oil in your skin to qualify you as an OPEC nation, or if you've got ravine-size acne gulches, use the oil-free or water-based stuff.

Take it from the guy who played Attila the Hun, even the "Scourge of God" is no match for the forces of nature. Regardless of whether you're in warm, humid weather or fighting the cold and wind, humectants in the moisturizer will keep your skin moist, so make sure you grease up before heading outdoors.

3 FIGHT WRINKLES

Overexposure to the sun will cause wrinkles faster than you can say, "Come back, Shane!"

To remain a softy, wear a broad-brimmed hat, some polarized shades, and a sunscreen with an SPF of at least 15. Apply the stuff liberally 15 to 30 minutes before going outside. Follow all these tips and you'll end up with skin that makes you feel young and confident. And confidence is sexy, don't you think?

How to Open Door #1, Door #2, or Door #3

Life is full of sticky jambs. What's the big deal?

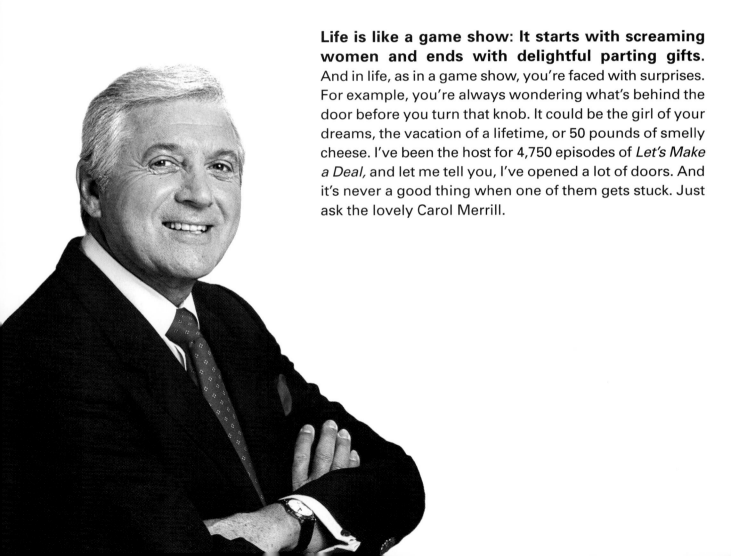

Life is like a game show: It starts with screaming women and ends with delightful parting gifts. And in life, as in a game show, you're faced with surprises. For example, you're always wondering what's behind the door before you turn that knob. It could be the girl of your dreams, the vacation of a lifetime, or 50 pounds of smelly cheese. I've been the host for 4,750 episodes of *Let's Make a Deal,* and let me tell you, I've opened a lot of doors. And it's never a good thing when one of them gets stuck. Just ask the lovely Carol Merrill.

1 IF A DOOR RESISTS OPENING, DON'T FORCE IT

You'll only scare the pygmy horses on the other side.

Instead, take a sheet of paper and slide it along the top and sides of the door. When the paper stops, you've hit your sticking point. If the door is stuck at the top on the knob side, tightening the screws on the lower hinge should make the door hang straighter. If it sticks at the bottom, tighten the top hinge. If that doesn't work, remove the door and shave down the sticking point with a hand plane, using long, smooth strokes. If none of these remedies works, your booby prize will be a bulky guy in a tool belt who'll clean out your wallet.

2 PATCH YOUR SCREEN DOOR

Just say to the nearest house-guest, "I'll give you $50 if you have a small piece of screening that matches my door."

Cut a patch about 2 inches larger on each side than the hole. If the screen is aluminum, remove a few wires from the edges of the patch and bend the remaining wires at a 90-degree angle. Center the patch on the hole,

poke the wires through the mesh, turn the whole screen over, and flatten. If the screen is fiberglass, lay the patch over the hole, align the patterns, apply a thin bead of adhesive around the edges, then blot off the excess.

3 LET'S SAY YOU'VE MADE A VERY GOOD DEAL

...and you're driving home in a brand-new car!

You wouldn't want the garage door to give it a nasty dent. To check your automatic garage-door

opener, stand outside the open door with your hands at waist level, ready to catch the door as it comes down. As the door falls into your hands [A], you should easily be able to stop it. If not, adjust the force-level control. (Check the instruction manual.) Next, put a 2-by-4 on the ground in the door's path [B]. When the door hits the stud, it should reverse direction. If it doesn't, adjust the door's close limit. (Back to the book.) Do it right, and you might save the lovely Carol Merrill's poodle from being squashed. That's a big deal any day.

How to Make a Quick Getaway

What do you do when you're standing over here, your horse is over there, and there's a whole heck of a lot of big trouble in between?

What you want in the worst way is to get to your horse, make a running mount, and clear out before the bullets start to fly. By the way, if you don't get this right the first time, you'll have a mighty powerful incentive to improve. You'll only miss that saddle three or four times before you get pretty accurate. And it sure helps if you know you've got a good horse. The first time I met Trigger, I wanted to know how good a horse he was, so I got on him and turned him. Well, he could spin on a dime and give you 9 cents back in change. We just fell in love. From then on, I never let him out of my sight. Finding a horse like Trigger is like finding a wife. The horse is your other half—he's your partner, and he can get you out of plenty of scrapes and close calls.

1 HOLD THE POMMEL AND RUN ALONGSIDE

The left-hand side, that is.

You'll need both hands on the saddle horn. Then, as the horse speeds up but before he reaches a gallop, kick your feet forward to a point alongside his front hooves. Plant your heels. Then, what with the momentum of the horse, you'll bounce up with your legs out behind you.

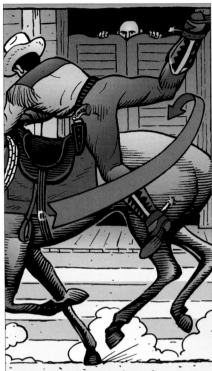

2 SWING YOUR LEG OVER AND LAND IN THE SADDLE

As you jump, the horse is in the right position for you to swing your right leg over the saddle.

This does take arm strength, of course, and you have to be able to keep yourself from going past the saddle and ending up on the far side of the horse. I always find that experience is a swell teacher.

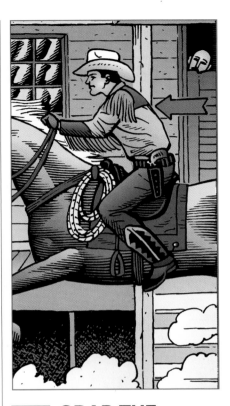

3 GRAB THE REINS, THEN FIND THE STIRRUPS

Leave the reins around the horse's neck, where you can reach them.

As you get better at mounting on the run, you'll do all three—land in the saddle, grab the reins, get your feet in the stirrups—at about the same time. But that's the order, in case something goes wrong.

uncommon *knowledge* *67*

How to Make Music out of Thin Air

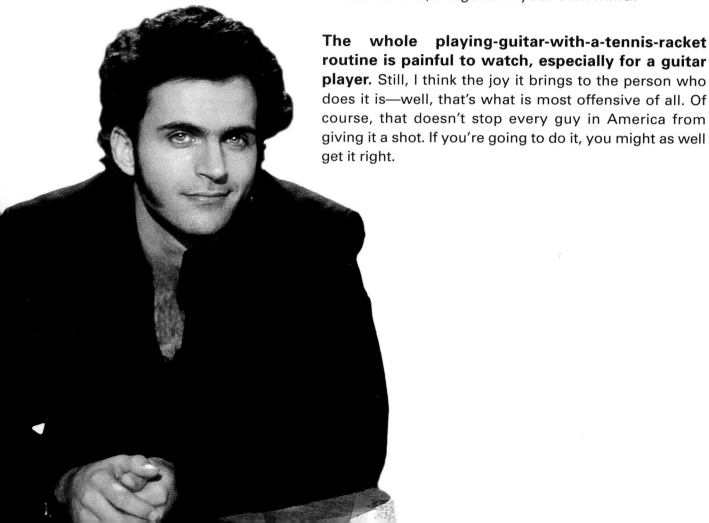

Sick day, a day all your own. The kids are at school, the wife's at MadMart. So you grab a copy of Springsteen's "Born to Run," jack the volume up to max, grab that invisible Stratocaster, and slide across the stage. Suddenly, you're the man with the mojo, the master of make-believe, a legend in your own mind!

The whole playing-guitar-with-a-tennis-racket routine is painful to watch, especially for a guitar player. Still, I think the joy it brings to the person who does it is—well, that's what is most offensive of all. Of course, that doesn't stop every guy in America from giving it a shot. If you're going to do it, you might as well get it right.

1 MAKE SURE YOU ACTUALLY HAVE AN AIR INSTRUMENT OF SOME KIND

Don't just flail around all over the place.

Coordinate your two hands so that one of them is where the picking hand should be and the other is where the hand that plays the notes should be. You have to visualize the neck of the guitar, its length and width, and where the high notes and low notes are. Next, listen to what's going on, so you don't overplay. Usually, amateur air guitarists get it all confused, because if they don't know how to do it, they figure the way to go is to make both hands do everything real fast. But that's the main problem. Don't overplay.

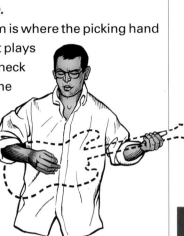

2 IF YOU'RE PLAYING LEAD, GOOD FACIAL GESTURES HELP

But watch out for the whammy bar.

A lot of people go wrong here because they lose the perception of the amount of force needed to work that little lever. The whammy gets a light touch [A]. Bend it too hard and you'll snap it right off. Another place where people often go way wrong is holding their hand too high on the neck [B]. Only a few high notes are played up there. Also, it helps to play these when actual high notes are occurring in the music. I've seen plenty of air guitarists play a wild flurry of music when somebody's just hit a chord or when there's no guitar happening at all. This might be a giveaway.

3 GAIN POINTS BY LOOKING LIKE A FAMOUS GUITAR PLAYER

For example, the Pete Townshend windmill thing—

or any of that jumping-around stuff—will gain good points, if only because if it looks at all like Pete, then somebody will say, "Hey! That's like Pete Townshend! And he's a guitar player. So you must be one, too." Mimicking somebody who is actually known as a guitar player will help create the image that you're also a famous guitarist. It's certainly better than just being some unknown nimrod playing air guitar.

PETE SAMPRAS

How to Make a Killing

Sometimes the buzz of trouble is everywhere. First it's the IRS, then it's your ex-wife, then a lousy housefly. It's time to take back your life. Slip into your exterminator whites, grab a swatter, and start with a pest you can control.

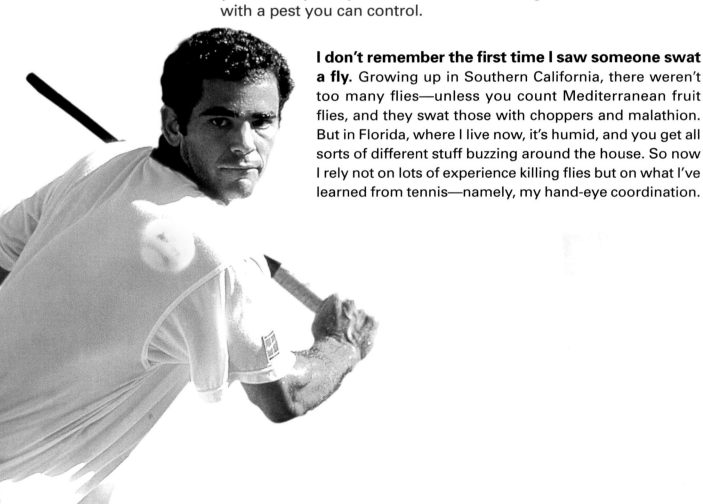

I don't remember the first time I saw someone swat a fly. Growing up in Southern California, there weren't too many flies—unless you count Mediterranean fruit flies, and they swat those with choppers and malathion. But in Florida, where I live now, it's humid, and you get all sorts of different stuff buzzing around the house. So now I rely not on lots of experience killing flies but on what I've learned from tennis—namely, my hand-eye coordination.

1 YOUR BRAIN IS BIGGER THAN A FLY'S

I've got a strong arm and it's pretty quick, and I've got a pretty strong wrist, but I'm also a lot smarter than a fly.

So I know better than to storm it. Instead, I use stealth and a good swatter. I use much more wrist in swatting a fly than in my tennis game, though. I recommend forehand swats, as opposed to backhands. I don't recommend using a racket to kill houseflies, though. Rackets are for outdoors: There are these big bumble-bees that come after me when I'm on the court here practicing, and when they come around, I can hit 'em pretty good with my racket. I use an overhead.

2 FOLLOW-THROUGH COUNTS

You can't hesitate for even a moment with flies. If you do, they're gone.

So when you go for the swat, swing right through the fly. If you try to hold back, it'll take away your edge. Go for oblivion, and worry about the cleanup later. If the fly escapes, track it down. Flies usually fly in squares (inset). Don't ask why. But that makes it a little easier to predict where they'll go next. Also, forget about body position when you're going for flies. It's more of a free-for-all thing.

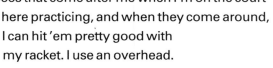

FLY TRAJECTORY

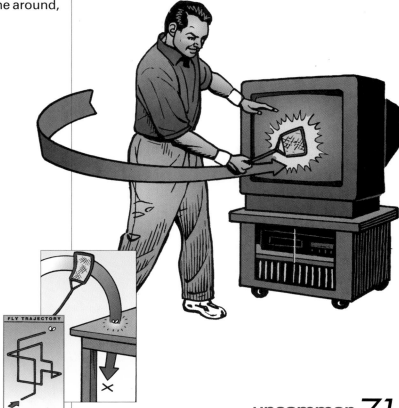

How to Soften the Blow

Life's full of little surprises. Some are nice, and some aren't. A smart guy will see the bad ones coming.

Let me define the sucker-punch concept for you: A sucker punch refers to a sucker being the recipient of a certain punch that he didn't know was coming. What you want to do is avoid being the recipient of that certain punch. How you do that is your business, but I can tell you how I do it, and I learned the hard way growing up in Washington, D.C. My old neighborhood was notorious for sucker punches. If you could spot one coming, you were at a decided advantage. Here's how not to be a sucker.

1 FIRST, ANALYZE THE SITUATION

If you know the signs to watch for, you can spot potential trouble.

When somebody's going to swing, he keeps a slight bend in his knees, since a good punch comes from the ground up. Another warning sign is that he keeps his hands down at his sides. Once you suspect that he's up to something, watch his face. He'll wait until you glance to one side or look off someplace before making a move. Don't let your gaze drop for even a nanosecond. Watch his eyes, especially. There's a certain intensity and stress in the eyes before a punch is thrown. Also, sometimes the nostrils flare or the guy grits his teeth or his lips get tight. Any of these things could mean trouble.

2 PREPARE TO REACT

An old martial-arts trick is to stand with your arms crossed in front of you or with one arm up so your fingers touch your chin or cheek.

It's a nonthreatening pose that's unlikely to provoke your antagonist, but it also gets your arms in a position to quickly deflect an incoming punch. Meanwhile, keep your distance. The guy may start edging a little closer. Don't let him. Stay at arm's length until you're sure he's ready to throw a punch.

3 IF HE MAKES HIS MOVE, DON'T TRY TO DUCK OUT OF RANGE

That will only give him room to take a full swing at you [A].

Instead, dive toward your opponent. If you're too close, he can't really hurt you. If you're a rightie, use your left arm to block the punch [B]. Keep your eye on the guy's fist. He'll probably go for your stomach, since, if you're paying attention, he won't be able to hit you in the face. It's a smaller target, and you can see the punch coming.

Whatever happens, alertness is the key. Even though it takes just a fraction of a second to throw a sucker punch, it takes less than that to duck one.

uncommon *knowledge* **73**

CHUCK YEAGER

How to Win a Dogfight

You never know when you're going to find yourself behind the wheel of an F-16—or maybe you do—but in case it ever does happen, here are the skills you need to master.

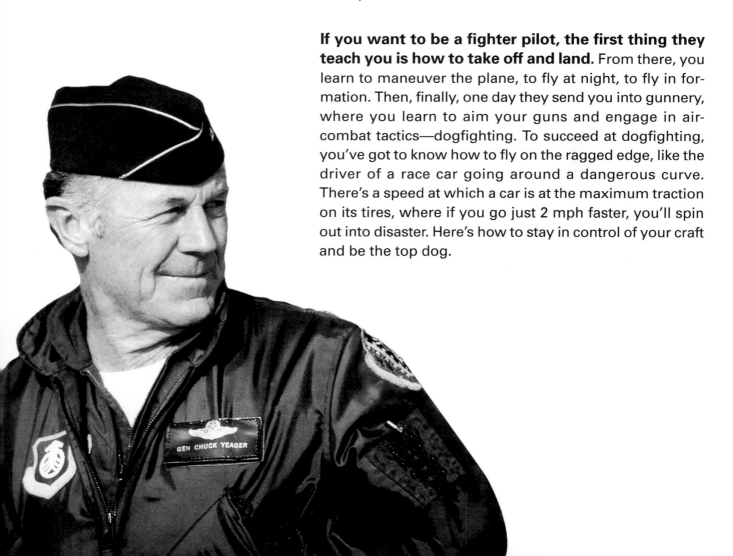

If you want to be a fighter pilot, the first thing they teach you is how to take off and land. From there, you learn to maneuver the plane, to fly at night, to fly in formation. Then, finally, one day they send you into gunnery, where you learn to aim your guns and engage in air-combat tactics—dogfighting. To succeed at dogfighting, you've got to know how to fly on the ragged edge, like the driver of a race car going around a dangerous curve. There's a speed at which a car is at the maximum traction on its tires, where if you go just 2 mph faster, you'll spin out into disaster. Here's how to stay in control of your craft and be the top dog.

1 | SEE MORE THAN YOUR OPPONENT SEES

If you're going to be a fighter pilot, you have to be alert to everything, whether at the horizon or swooping down from behind cloud cover.

Now, if you shut your eyes, relax, then open them again, you'll automatically focus to about 18 feet. That's normal. But in a dogfight, naturally you've got to be able to see a lot farther. The trick is to [A] look down at the ground so you're taking in about a 50-to-80-mile piece of real estate. When you've got that in focus, [B] lift your eyes back to the sky. You've now taken your focus to infinity and back again, and you should be able to see anything else in the sky around you.

2 | FLY THE BULLET

Once you learn to see, you can learn to shoot.

The object of dogfighting is to get your guns pointed at the right place. You have to shoot the bullets far enough ahead of the other pilot

that the bullets and his plane converge on the same place at the same time. In order to lead the other plane, you have to be able to make your aircraft an extension of your body. Don't even think about turning. Just turn your head or your body and let the plane come along for the ride. When you take aim, fly the bullet into position.

3 | USE ALL FOUR DIMENSIONS

The average pilot thinks in terms of three dimensions— length, width, height.

But in a dogfight, a precise sense of time becomes just as important. What most pilots don't realize is that by controlling the throttle, they're controlling time—how long it takes to travel from point A to point B. This sense of how you and your opponent exist in time and space comes into play strategically in combat. For example, when the guy you're tailing suddenly cuts back his power, you've got to sense it right away or you'll fly right past him and become the prey instead of the hunter.

HANK WILLIAMS JR.

How to Fill a 10-Gallon Hat

"Use your head," your mama said. But how? Well, you can shave it. Or you can lose it over the wrong person. Or you can use it to keep your hat off your shoulders.

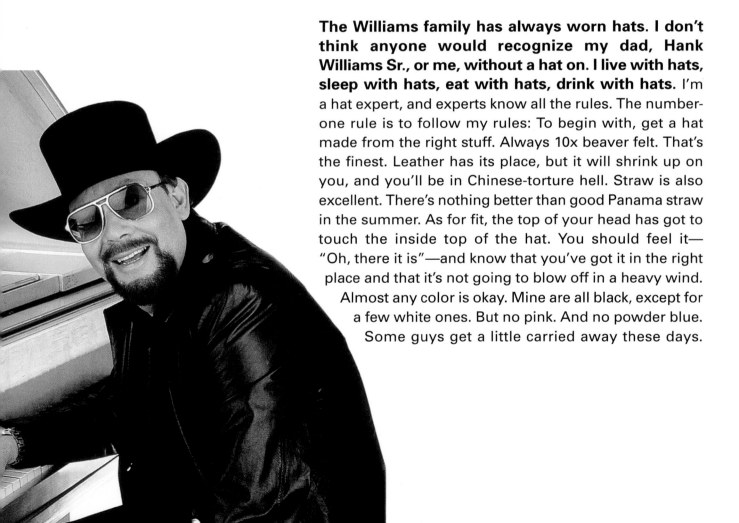

The Williams family has always worn hats. I don't think anyone would recognize my dad, Hank Williams Sr., or me, without a hat on. I live with hats, sleep with hats, eat with hats, drink with hats. I'm a hat expert, and experts know all the rules. The number-one rule is to follow my rules: To begin with, get a hat made from the right stuff. Always 10x beaver felt. That's the finest. Leather has its place, but it will shrink up on you, and you'll be in Chinese-torture hell. Straw is also excellent. There's nothing better than good Panama straw in the summer. As for fit, the top of your head has got to touch the inside top of the hat. You should feel it— "Oh, there it is"—and know that you've got it in the right place and that it's not going to blow off in a heavy wind. Almost any color is okay. Mine are all black, except for a few white ones. But no pink. And no powder blue. Some guys get a little carried away these days.

1 GET A HAT WITH THE RIGHT BRIM

Don't get a little 2-inch brim, so water won't run down the back of your neck.

To help keep rain off you and your coat, you need a brim that's big enough to make a difference. By the way, don't wreck a good hat with a stupid hatband. Whatever you do, please don't buy one of those ridiculous, ugly feather hatbands.

2 CONSIDER WHAT YOU'RE PUTTING IT ON

Pick out a hat that works with the shape of your head.

A guy with a thin face [A] should have an RCA crown—that's a Rodeo Cowboy Association crown, which is narrow with a crease on top and a flat brim. Guys with moon heads [B] look bad in hats with little, skinny brims. Bad idea. Go for a hat with a wider brim. If you've got an

oval-shaped head or a big, square jaw [C], the cowboy hat you usually see in the movies will do fine. You need an ample-sized hat. Keep the crown low; you can turn the brim up more than usual. Never wear the damn thing straight on—unless you're a really big guy, a 6'5" guy [D]. If a big guy wears a black one straight on, à la Billy Jack, it looks good—and even if it doesn't, you're not going to say a damn word to him about it anyway. The rest of us need a hat with a little cockiness off to the side. I tilt mine to the right.

3 ONCE YOU GET THE RIGHT HAT, CARE FOR IT PROPERLY

Never take it off your head, except at funerals.

Never put your hat on a chair in a restaurant if you have friends who are NFL football players. Derrick Thomas, the Kansas City Chiefs' linebacker, sat on my hat. I hated him for doing that. If you do have to put your hat down, there's only one way: It's crown down. There's not a choice. If you lay it down flat, onto the brim, gravity will take over, and if you leave it long enough, you'll look like a Mennonite, and that look is not in right now. One last thing: Don't leave your hat on the dashboard of your pickup truck. The sun will just ruin it.

YES NO

AL UNSER JR.

How to Take Your Turn

A lot of life consists of waiting for your moment, that instant when what you've been doing is nothing like what you're going to be doing. Sometimes, in fact, there's a whole lot of excitement waiting for you right around the next bend.

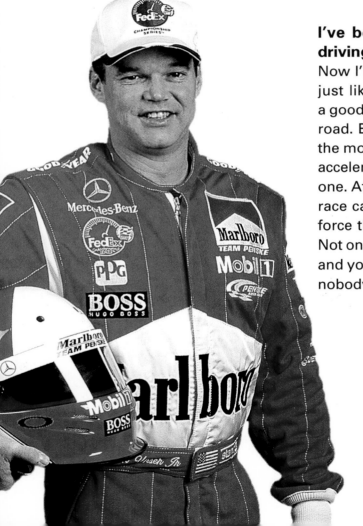

I've been racing almost my whole life. I started driving go-carts when I was 9. My father taught me. Now I'm teaching my son. I explain these things to him just like my dad explained them to me. I tell him that a good driver loves a straight line, especially on a curving road. Each corner is different. You drive into it, wait for the moment when the car starts to break away, lift off the accelerator, then accelerate again and head for the next one. After a while, you just feel it. Passenger cars are not race cars, of course. On a track, you can let centrifugal force throw you out of a curve and into a straightaway. Not on a mountain road. Cut a curve too wide or too tight, and you're driving on the "marbles"—the gravel—where nobody runs.

1 STRAIGHTEN OUT THE TURN

My father showed me how to take a corner by straightening it out, and how to use the entire road to loosen up a tight turn.

The trick is to get to the far outside edge of your lane as you approach the turn [A]. Then point the car toward the inside edge of the lane at the apex of the turn [B], letting the inside front tire almost nick the shoulder of the road. As you come out of the turn, drift to the outside of the lane again [C]. For best control, avoid braking when you're actually in the turn. Think ahead and trim some speed before you enter the bend in the road, and put off any acceleration until you have a fairly straight line ahead of you (shown as x and y below).

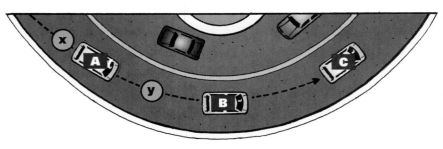

2 GET A BEAD ON YOUR TARGET

You control the corner better if you break it into two parts: entry-to-inside-edge-of-turn and inside-of-turn-to-exit.

Use your eyes to do this. As you enter the corner turn, draw an imaginary line right to your target [D]. Keep as close to it as possible for best control.

Once you've got the car aimed in the right direction, look for your exit point. That's the sequence: Pick your line, turn, pick your next line, turn. Don't look and turn at the same time. Good drivers must be able to disconnect their hands and eyes.

3 DON'T OVERSTEER

You don't have to turn the wheel as hard as you think.

In a race car, drivers never move the steering wheel more than a quarter-turn, and even then we do it slowly. Most people spin the steering wheel too freely and too hard, and the result is an inefficient turn. For best control of the wheel, keep your elbows tucked to your sides [E], then lean into the turn, using your whole upper body for control [F].

How to Be Cool in Shades

Nothing like a big stink of heat and a pile of midsummer sunlight to make you wish you could draw the drapes, slap on a recording of "Georgia," and think long, nasty, very cool thoughts of how nice life would be if only the lights were just a little lower.

Look, I don't know anything about the cool thing. I only know what works for me. I cannot be, uh, anyone but myself. If I'm cool, that's cool. If I'm not cool, that's cool, too. For me, sunglasses are cool because I wear them. If I didn't wear them, I wouldn't think they were cool. If you want to wear them, wear the ones that suit your style.

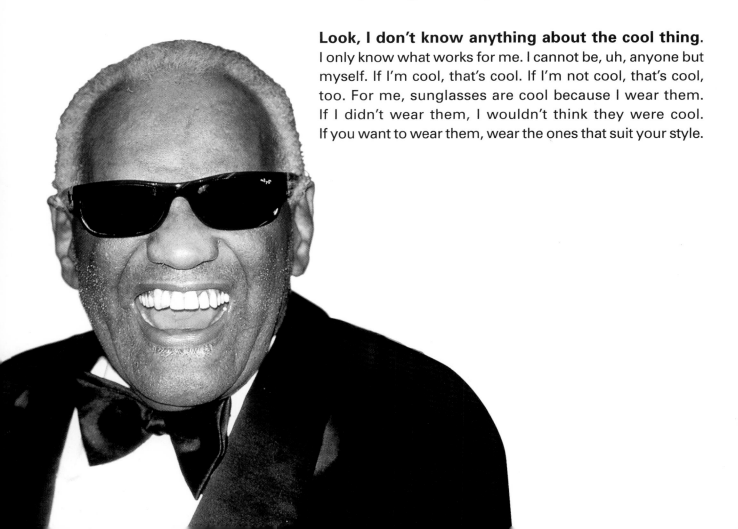

1 GET A GOOD FIT

Some of the guys in the band accuse me of directing the orchestra with my head.

There was even one wigged-out reporter who said I directed it with my feet. I do move around a lot at the keyboard, and the band takes their cue from that, so my glasses have to stay on my head. But they can't be too tight. They have to feel right, see what I mean? So check the pressure points—the temples and the bridge. Don't be afraid to try some different things before you settle on the thing that makes sense for you. For a while there, I wore those wraparound sunglasses. It was an experiment. How are you gonna know if you like steak when you're eatin' spaghetti every night? Try the steak, baby!

2 GET A SECOND OPINION

Trusted advisors can help you pin down your style.

These days, I have, you know, what they call a retinue, and my valet is in charge of all my needs, accoutrements, clothes, and so on. And he pretty much knows what I like. For example, now I wear horn-rims with extra-wide side pieces almost all the time. Why? They just feel good. I found that the ones that look best are the ones that feel the best, see? I figure, be the person that you wanna be, and that's the coolest person you're ever gonna be.

3 GET TO KNOW YOUR STYLE

I used to wear all kinds of sunglasses, just like I used to sing like Nat King Cole.

People used to say of me, "Damn, he sure do sound like Nat King Cole." But there came a day, and luckily for me it was early, when I woke up and asked myself, "Well, when are they gonna ask me to sing because I sound like me?" So my advice is, never do anything you don't like. For instance, I never liked those aviator-type sunglasses, because they weren't me, see?

Paramilitary shades are cool by intimidation—the law's on your side.

Classic horn-rims give you that bad-boy Jack Nicholson look.

Nothing says "Terminator!" like wraparound Arnold shades.

You don't need sun to wear shades. Ray Bans indoors lend mystery.

GEORGE STEPHANOPOULOS

How to Tell Which Way the Wind Blows

When it comes to politics, everybody wants to know where the next storm's coming from. That makes being a good weatherman a valuable asset.

Here's how I discovered the importance of political meteorology: In 1983, I was 22 and working as an aide for an Ohio congressman. When Reagan invaded Grenada, I thought it was terrible. So the next morning I got up at six, went in to the office, and typed a speech for my boss on how the invasion was the worst thing in the world. Then I sold it to my boss. I said, "Listen, Reagan's never going to get away with this. He'll definitely get beat in '84, and he may even get impeached." Unfortunately, my boss took my advice and gave the speech. That's when I learned how carefully you have to read the skies.

1 TEST THE WINDS

There are three basic kinds of wind-readers.

My old partner, James Carville, is a low-tech kind of guy. He's Mr. Finger-in-the-Wind. Newt Gingrich, on the other hand, is an information-age guy, so I think he'd go for an electronic weather vane. Me, I come down on the side of the wind sock. A wind sock can tell you not only how the wind is blowing, but also whether there's a storm on the way. To make one, get a pair of panty hose and cut off one leg. Cut out a golf ball–size hole in the toe. Then use glue to attach the thigh to a lightweight dog collar or a strip of clear plastic—like the stuff around the collar of a new shirt—with the ends stuck together to make a ring. Or cut a strip out of a plastic file folder and stick the ends together. Next, poke a hole in your plastic ring at the top and another, directly opposite, at the bottom. Slide a small rod—a fishing pole works best—through the holes, so the sock will turn easily with the wind.

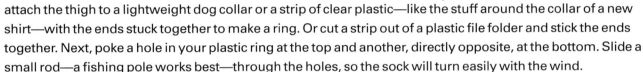

2 TAKE A SAFE POSITION

While you want to mount your sock in an open area away from tall buildings, putting it on top of a building is a great idea.

If you want to plant a wind-sock pole, the rule of thumb is to measure the height of the nearest tall building, multiply by three, and place your sock that far away from it. Special note of caution to political wind-readers: To avoid false readings, don't mount your sock too close to the podium.

60'

180'

3 LOOK OUT FOR STORMS

A good wind sock will tell you which way the wind's blowing, and also how hard.

When your sock is fully extended, you can figure a wind speed of more than 17 mph. Winds from the west usually mean fair weather, but if they're coming from the east, watch for a storm in the next 48 hours—sooner if the barometer's falling! Remember: "Winds from the east suit neither man nor beast." Storms blowing out of the northeast are more threatening and, in the winter, likely to bring snow. And really bad weather always hampers turnout at the polls.

VIDAL SASSOON

How to Dig Your Way out of Trouble

Sure, you may be able to hit a Jimmy Key fastball, direct Julia Roberts, or even trim the bangs of the rich and famous. But what are you going to do when you finally have to get a real job?

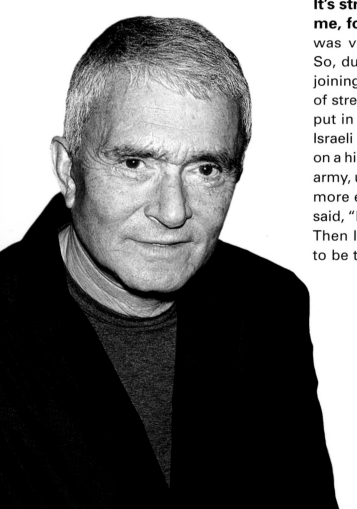

It's strange how you come by an honest trade. Take me, for example. By 1948, I was 20, a young Jew who was very angry about what had gone on in Europe. So, during that period of my hairdressing career, I was joining antifascist groups in London and getting into a lot of street action where people were getting arrested and put in jail. Eventually, I felt it might be safer to join the Israeli army. I was wrong. Within 2 months, I was hidden on a hillside behind Arab lines, surrounded by the Egyptian army, under attack from dive-bombers and artillery. It was more excitement than I ever expected. Then somebody said, "Hey, you! Dig a ditch!" I said, "Who, me? I cut hair." Then I looked around. Ditch digging suddenly seemed to be the career move of choice. Here's what I learned.

1 KNOW YOUR TOOLS

Spades [A] are for digging. Shovels [B] are for scooping.

Don't try to dig a hole with a shovel. If you have to choose, go for a spade over a shovel, since a spade can shovel, but a shovel can't spade. Normally sensible men become ditch-digging idiots when they first try to dig a hole. Why? Because they grab a spade and start digging, then fall apart after scratching around in the rocks for a few hours. Don't waste time trying to jam a spade into a piece of rocky soil. Break it up with a pick or mattock [C], then use a spade or shovel to remove the loosened dirt. If necessary, break it up some more.

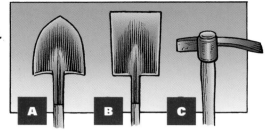

2 GET A GRIP

Hold the tool right for proper leverage.

If you're right-handed, put your right hand as far up on the handle of the spade as possible [D], but not so far that it's uncomfortable. Your left hand should be about 18 inches down the handle [E]. Then use your legs. Not your back, and not your shoulder. Push with your left leg and right arm. If you're using a spade to cut into the earth, don't fool around; use all your body weight to get the spade as deep as possible. Jump on it.

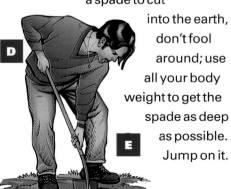

3 WATCH YOUR BACK

A little footwork will protect you from injury.

Once you're loaded up [F], pivot your feet [G] to dump the load. If you twist your back instead, you're liable to hurt yourself.

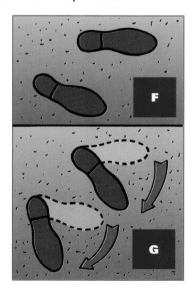

4 UNDERSTAND EXCAVATION

There's a certain architecture to a hole in the ground.

A good, safe 4-foot-deep hole or ditch is 12 to 18 inches wider at the top than at the bottom. So if you want a 4-foot-deep trench with a 12-inch floor, you'll have at least a 2-foot opening at the top—unless you don't mind the walls collapsing.

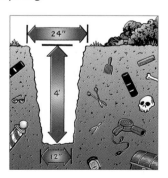

MICKEY SPILLANE

How to Case a Joint

Sometimes the big-ticket items you buy can reach up and grab you around the throat like a dope-crazed fiend in a blind alley. Choosing a house can be like that. It's the kind of thing that makes even the toughest man in the world say, "Eeek!"

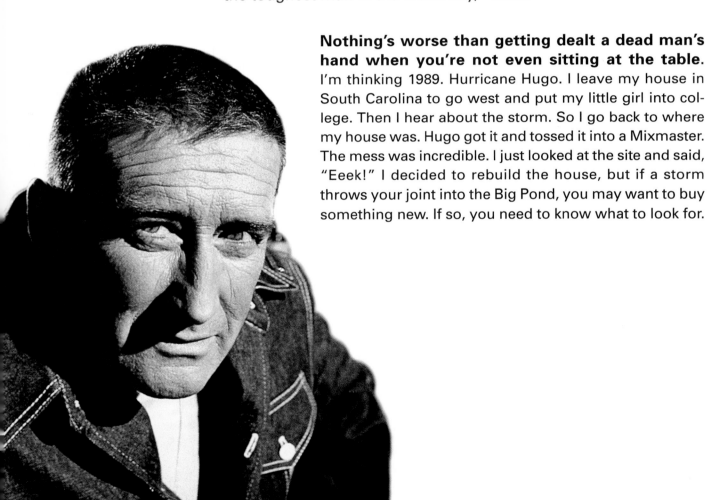

Nothing's worse than getting dealt a dead man's hand when you're not even sitting at the table. I'm thinking 1989. Hurricane Hugo. I leave my house in South Carolina to go west and put my little girl into college. Then I hear about the storm. So I go back to where my house was. Hugo got it and tossed it into a Mixmaster. The mess was incredible. I just looked at the site and said, "Eeek!" I decided to rebuild the house, but if a storm throws your joint into the Big Pond, you may want to buy something new. If so, you need to know what to look for.

1. KNOW WHERE THE BODIES ARE BURIED

While the dames yak in the kitchen, you head to the cellar.

The dead bodies of a house— the rotten floor joists, leaky plumbing, and potentially bad wiring— are all buried in the basement. Look there first, and if you don't like what you see, say, "So long, sucker. Not for me." While you're down there, look around for leaky pipes [A] and check the wood for signs of decay wherever it comes in contact with the concrete, such as floor joists supported on concrete walls [B]; framing supported in a pocket in a concrete wall [C]; and wood posts supported on a concrete floor [D].

2. STAKE OUT THE NEIGHBORS

Are they flaky?

Do they have a dozen kennels in the backyard? What are the colors of the local gangs? (Be careful if they wear pastels.) If you find a place in town, look at the block. You'll want the worst house on the nicest block (at right); the value of your place will go up as you work on it. If you choose the best place on a rotten block, you'll have to improve everybody else's houses to make yours worth squat.

3. LOOK FOR CLUES

Does the bank manager laugh out loud when you tell him what you want to buy?

Are there water marks on the ceiling over the toilet bowl? Are there bloodstains on the floorboards? Do you see a high-water mark in the basement? These are all bad signs. Some good ones? Here are two ways to find a bargain:

- Hang out at the courthouse. Wait for the cops to grab a con by his white collar for a money crime. Ask the guy if he wants to sell. He may need the cash.
- Read the obits. Find somebody who died violently in a nice house (at right). The house'll go cheap— and once you've cleaned up the mess, you can live with a legend.

HARRY ANDERSON

How to Make Money on the Street

Michael Milken did it his way, Bill Gates did it another way, and Roger Altman did it yet another way. In America, it seems, anybody can make a buck on Wall Street. All it takes is guts and a system—and a very good game.

There's only one way to win the shell game: Be the dealer, not a player, because if you play, you lose. Why? Because it's not a game of skill. It's a game of money, and whoever runs the game takes the money. In New Orleans, I used to run a shell game, and we had a saying: The dealer has three shells—one for the guy who knows nothing about the game, another for the wise guy who thinks he knows, and a third for the pea. Years later, when I volunteered to be a poster boy for a New York City campaign against street cons, the mayor wouldn't pose with me because I had a bunco rap. But it's all show biz. The games you see on the street are like little playlets, each with its own cast of players. You've got your tosser (the dealer), your shills (those are the only players who win), and the two guys who work behind the scenes— the lookout and the muscle.

1 WATCH THE OTHER SHELL

In the shell game, only the tosser, or dealer [A], knows where the pea is.

The two shills [B and C] are there to stir up some excitement and maybe win a few games to convince the honest player [D] that the game is on the level. The lookout [E] checks the street for the cops. The guy we don't see is the muscle, whose job it is to get the dealer's money back should the player actually win.

2 NO, NO, THE OTHER SHELL

Let's say we've got shells A, B, and C.

The pea starts under shell A, and I do a little dance and I move the shells around. Now, the average citizen is going to watch that shell. Shell A is for him. Then we've got shell B. As I do my little dance, I make a little,

almost imperceptible tweak (inset) with my finger under shell B. I do this for the poor sap who knows the game's rigged and thinks I've stolen the pea from under shell A—which, in fact, I have. But I'm not putting it under shell B like he thinks. I'm concealing it in shell C. What can I say? Life is ugly.

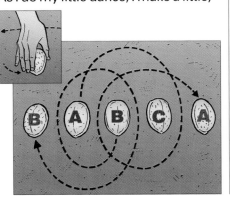

3 KEEP TRYING

As I said, shell C, which no one has even seen me touch, is where I've stashed the pea.

It's been under there a while—since my little song and dance started, in fact. Shell C doesn't get picked often. It's for the complete nincompoop, the guy who plays blind. He doesn't follow shell A, and he figures nobody would actually cheat. That leaves him with a one-in-three chance of doubling his money, if he's lucky. If he's lucky a lot, however, there's a guy waiting for him around the corner ready to help reestablish the odds in the dealer's favor. So, really, the bottom line is, if you want to gamble, this isn't the game for you: There's absolutely no risk of winning.

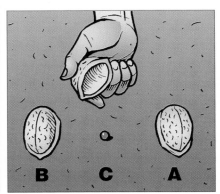

How to Give a Speech

They say public speaking is the most stressful thing a man can do with his clothes on. No surprise: In a roomful of strangers, you're not only the only one talking; you're also the only one facing the wrong way. It's no time to find yourself speechless, and no time to clown around.

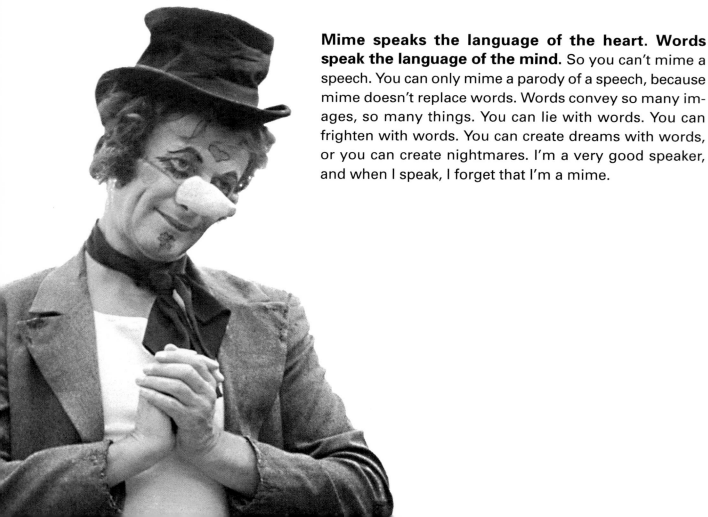

Mime speaks the language of the heart. Words speak the language of the mind. So you can't mime a speech. You can only mime a parody of a speech, because mime doesn't replace words. Words convey so many images, so many things. You can lie with words. You can frighten with words. You can create dreams with words, or you can create nightmares. I'm a very good speaker, and when I speak, I forget that I'm a mime.

1 KEEP YOUR HANDS TO YOURSELF

Use gestures, but simply.

Nobody likes somebody who talks too much, so don't talk a lot with your hands. Don't wave your arms, and don't make too many sweeping gestures with your hands. Also, don't roll your eyes, or people will think you're crazy.

- A palms-up gesture [A] is warm and welcoming. If it's part of a gesture in which you also move your hand away from your body, it suggests nonthreatening explanation.
- Use finger-pointing [B] sparingly. Too much jabbing at the air and you look ugly and pugnacious.
- Your palm is not an anvil [C]. If you use this gesture repeatedly, you'll turn giving a speech into an act of manual labor.
- If you run out of words, you can always keep moving your lips while pressing your palms against the invisible glass wall separating you from your audience [D].

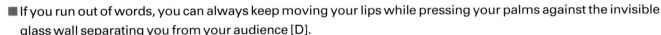

2 WATCH WHERE YOU'RE TALKING

When you're standing in front of an audience, you can't ignore them any more than they can ignore you.

Look at them. If this intimidates you, choose two or three places out in the crowd—maybe one just off-center, maybe one in the back—and let your eyes keep returning to those spots.

The effect on the audience will be that you'll appear to connect what you are saying with those to whom you are speaking.

3 KEEP A STIFF UPPER TORSO

It's not just what you say that makes a speech great, it's how you say it.

Stand up straight; lean in. Your posture says a lot. How can you give a stirring speech if you're slouching in defeat? Move your body for emphasis, but don't dance around. Remember, when you make a gesture or a posture change, you're moving your whole body. To the audience, the whole image in front of them changes. Great speakers know this. So do great mimes.

Photography Credits